Eliza

"Did yo
Eliza?" C

"Yes, I ... was a splendid program, especially the carol arrangements. I had a lovely time."

"Good. I was hoping perhaps you'd consider attending another similar concert with me two evenings hence."

She felt Micah's and Anabelle's eyes center on her. Eliza had told Ana before arranging this outing that she had no desire to begin keeping regular company with young men. Charles, it was true, had been the ultimate gentleman, and she really didn't want to encourage him. But neither did she wish to offend him. "Well, I—"

A shadow fell across their table as someone approached. "Why, Eliza!" a deep voice exclaimed. "What a surprise."

As her gaze swung up to that very familiar face, she felt all the color drain from her own. "W–Weston!" All but choking on the name, she sprang to her feet, toppling her chair in her haste. All thought vanished but one: escape.

SALLY LAITY has successfully written several novels, including a coauthored series for Tyndale, three Barbour novellas, and six Heartsongs. Her favorite thing these days is counseling new authors via the Internet. Sally always loved to write, and after her four children were grown she took college writing courses and attended Christian writing conferences. She has written both historical and contemporary romances and considers it a joy to know that the Lord can touch other hearts through her stories. She makes her home in Bakersfield, California, with her husband and enjoys being a grandma.

Books by Sally Laity

HEARTSONG PRESENTS
HP4—Reflections of the Heart
HP31—Dream Spinner
HP81—Better Than Friends
HP236—Valiant Heart
HP311—If the Prospect Pleases

Little Shoes and Mistletoe

Sally Laity

Heartsong Presents

To Sarah Katherine and Grace Abigail,
my two newest angels.
Special thanks to Dianna and Gloria.

A note from the author:
I love to hear from my readers! You may correspond with me by writing:

Sally Laity
Author Relations
PO Box 719
Uhrichsville, OH 44683

ISBN 1-57748-699-4

LITTLE SHOES AND MISTLETOE

All Scripture quotations are taken from the Authorized King James Version of the Bible.

Cover illustration by Lisa Peruchini.

PRINTED IN THE U.S.A.

one

New York, 1898

New-fallen snow transformed Manhattan into a magical fairyland, hushed and glorious and glistening in the November sunshine like millions of diamonds scattered by an unseen hand. Every object in view sported a coating of frothy whiteness. Even the bottommost branches of the twin hemlocks out front drooped beneath the heavy blanket. Admiring the charming Currier & Ives scene from the parlor window of Harper House, Eliza Criswell almost forgot her melancholy.

"Quite peaceful, considering the way the wind howled around us half the night," her aunt Phoebe Harper said as she swept into the room, the hem of her russet morning gown swishing softly over the emerald and gold carpet.

Dragging her gaze from winter's unexpected but breathtaking spectacle, Eliza released the lace undercurtain and turned to her widowed aunt with a thin smile, the best she could muster. "Oh. You've brought breakfast. You should have let me carry that tray for you, Auntie."

"Nonsense." The birdlike woman shrugged beneath the crocheted shawl draping her shoulders. "This old body of mine might have a few aches and pains now and again, but I'm not completely infirm yet." Resting the edge of the silver tray on one of two lace-covered tables gracing the bright front room, she removed the coffee carafe and other accouterments that gleamed in the warm glow from the crackling fire.

Eliza helped set out embossed napkins, utensils, and china plates bearing warm, cranberry-raisin scones, then flicked a glance around her aunt's combination tea parlor and gift shop. An assortment of cabinets and shelves fairly overflowed with tasteful, handcrafted items of particular interest to women. "What if customers come while we're eating?"

Aunt Phoebe remained nonplused. "It takes awhile for folks to clear their walks after a sudden snow. One of my greatest blessings is having young Peter Bradley living next door. That boy has taken it upon himself to look after me since my beloved Captain Harper went down at sea. I think the world of him; I surely do. If I'd had a son of my own. . ." A slight sigh punctuated the unfinished thought.

Eliza recalled the shoveling sounds that had drifted to her second-floor bedroom while she dressed. "How thoughtful. I've often wondered how you managed after Uncle Amos passed on. Even though New York and Pennsylvania share a common border, Manhattan might as well be in Europe, the way Father's business affairs prevented our family from traveling. I'd have loved being able to visit you more often."

"Yes, well, the good Lord never forgets His own." She gestured for Eliza to be seated, then took the needlepoint-cushioned chair opposite her. "And the people at church take His instructions to heart, too. They see that the widows of the flock are cared for."

"Sounds like a splendid congregation. I shall look forward to attending services with you."

The older woman nodded and reached out to take Eliza's hand for grace.

The feeling of the frail, gnarled fingers caught at Eliza's heart. Upon her arrival yesterday, she'd been shocked to see how much her aunt had aged in the last ten years. Though Aunt Phoebe remained spry for the ripe old age of sixty-four, even the most casual observer could detect her occasional halting step, the slower movements which quickly sapped her energy. Eliza well understood the reason she had received the recent invitation to come live with her aunt.

It couldn't have arrived at a more opportune time, either,

Eliza conceded bitterly, slamming mental doors shut against an assault of painful memories. When the realization dawned that her aunt had finished praying, she smoothed the napkin over the lap of her sapphire gown and met the faded blue eyes across the table. "How long have you been running a gift shop, Aunt Phoebe?"

The older woman sipped her coffee and set down the fragile cup. "Oh, about two years now. It seemed an excellent way of supplying niceties for special occasions. Not that I need the extra income, you understand. The Captain left me quite comfortable, even with the expenses it takes to keep up Harper House. But I like to be able to give regularly to the needy. Orphans in the city, to be more precise."

Such selflessness touched Eliza. "But where do you get all the beautiful stock? Everywhere I look I see something exquisite—porcelain dolls, intricately scrolled stationery, crocheted furniture scarves, handmade lace. Wherever do you find such a lovely selection?"

"I make it."

Eliza stopped chewing and touched her napkin to the corners of her lips. "All of this?"

"That's right, dear. When a body spends so much time alone, there are scores of empty hours to fill. From the time I was a young wife, coping with solitude when the Captain was off at sea, I would pull my rocking chair close to the hearth and work on whatever new project happened to catch my fancy at the time. Some of my handiwork I gave to friends on birthdays and what have you, but over the years I accumulated far too much for personal use. Then the thought came to me to open a little shop." She paused. "Of course, my stock always dwindles rapidly as Christmas nears. I'm hoping now that you've come, you might learn a few skills, help me keep up with the demand."

"I'd be delighted." The possibility of becoming accomplished at those arts appealed to Eliza's own creative nature.

Her gaze drifted once more to the decorative objects.

Aunt Phoebe nodded and took another sip of coffee. "Did you sleep well with that storm carrying on outside?"

"Oh, yes. I must have been more tired than I realized after the train trip. And the feather bed in your front bedroom is simply delightful."

"Well, I'm just glad to have you here. I've been rattling around this big place by myself much too long." She finished the last bite of her scone, her shrewd eyes peering kindly at Eliza through rimless eyeglasses. "I know it was not the happiest of occasions that made you willing to leave Harrisburg, my dear."

Eliza felt a stinging in the back of her eyes and averted her attention to the cup she held.

"But if it brought you to me," her aunt went on, "it must have been part of God's mysterious workings. Perhaps when you're up to talking about things, you'll feel free to confide in your old auntie. These bony shoulders may not look like much, but they'll do for a good cry now and again."

Giving a perfunctory nod, Eliza managed to swallow the remainder of her scone.

The front door opened just then, emitting a blast of icy air, and the silver bell suspended above the entrance trilled the arrival of a customer.

Glancing toward the visitor as her aunt rose, Eliza did a double take, almost choking on a sip of hot coffee. For a second the man had looked exactly like—she swallowed more calmly—*Weston*. A wave of nausea raged through her at the feasibility that Weston Elliot might have had the gall to follow her. She sloughed off the foolish pounding of her heart and stood to begin clearing the table.

"Good morning, my dear Mrs. Harper," came the newcomer's cheery voice.

"And good day to you, Micah. Right on time, as always."

"Just trying to match your faithfulness," he said smoothly.

"And it's on my way, actually, to my first call."

"I'll just get this week's money from the drawer. How have things been going?"

"Surprisingly well, until I find myself suddenly frustrated and rebuffed at every turn. But we can't afford to give up, not when there's so much dire need."

From time to time during the exchange, Eliza sensed his gaze move to her. And linger. Still shaken by the mistaken notion of his identity, she almost lost hold of the cut-glass sugar bowl she was about to set on the tray. Taking a firmer grip on the handle, she put it in place, then reached for the matching cream pitcher.

"Oh, Micah," Eliza heard her aunt say. "You haven't met my new housemate. She just arrived yesterday from Harrisburg and will be living with me now."

"Is that right?" he asked politely.

"Eliza, come here, dear," the older woman said. "There's someone I'd like to introduce to you."

Chagrined that she hadn't quite made her escape to the kitchen, Eliza cringed. Nevertheless, setting her burden back down, she acted the dutiful young niece and approached the two with an aloof smile.

"Micah," Aunt Phoebe said, gesturing with one arm, "I'd like to present my favorite niece, Miss Eliza Grace Criswell. Eliza, this is Micah Richmond from my church. He works with Child Placement Services, a true servant of the Lord."

"Miss Criswell." He took Eliza's hand and bowed over it gallantly. "It's a pleasure to meet a relative of this wonderful lady. She's been extremely unselfish in support of my work, and I'm not alone in the great admiration I feel for her."

Finally raising her lashes, Eliza met the young man's eyes. The identical light brown she'd dreaded stared back at her, and they were even framed in a squarish face. Quite startling, even unnerving, the similarity between this man and that wretched Weston. Realizing she was gawking at him in a most unladylike fashion, Eliza reclaimed her fingers and moistened her lips. "Pleased to meet you."

"And I you. I hope you enjoy New York City. A touch larger than Pennsylvania's fine capital, but it has its friendly side, as I'm sure you'll discover."

"Y–yes, I'm sure," she stammered while a few more pertinent details registered. *Hair that same shade of sandy brown, corresponding height and bearing. . .*

"Eliza." Aunt Phoebe's voice broke into her reverie. "Is there more coffee left in the carafe? I'm sure Micah would like to warm up before going back outside into the cold."

"Oh, no, no." He raised his hand. "Thank you for the offer, ladies, but I'm afraid I'll be late for my appointment if I tarry a minute more. Next time, perhaps?" Pocketing the contribution the older woman had given him, he tipped his head respectfully. "Mrs. Harper. As always, I'm grateful for your boundless generosity." He then smiled at Eliza. "A pleasure meeting you, Miss Criswell. No doubt we'll see one another at Sunday services, to say nothing of my future visits here."

"No doubt," she parroted with a slight nod. "Mr. Richmond."

Plunking his felt bowler atop his thick light brown hair, he turned toward the door and took his leave, setting the little bell to tinkling again. His descending footfalls echoed from the wooden porch steps, fading into the distance.

"A fine, fine young man, that one," Aunt Phoebe remarked. "He has a deep burden for the immigrant children in the tenements and works night and day trying to find homes for little ones who've been orphaned by the rampant diseases."

"You don't say. Aren't there orphan asylums in the city?" Hoping that conversation would help her to gather herself, Eliza returned to the table for the breakfast tray.

"Several. And every one of them bulging at the seams with forlorn and destitute youngsters. It's a fair shame, that's what it is, but we do what we can to help." She heaved a thoughtful sigh, then gave Eliza a thin smile. "Well, if you don't mind washing up those dishes, I'll dust the shop and see which of my handicrafts seem in the shortest supply. We'll start that lesson first."

"Fine, Auntie. I won't be long."

Once in the solitude of the roomy kitchen, Eliza carried the breakfast things to the sideboard, grateful for an opportunity to calm nerves frazzled by the visitor's uncanny resemblance to her former fiancé. At her first glimpse of the man, a wave of nausea had surged through her. Thankfully that had subsided as quickly as it had come.

She sank to the seat of the nearest spindle-backed chair, her gaze idly reacquainting herself with the massive coal stove, the polished wood floor, and the ruffled chintz curtains gracing the double window. Everything appeared tidy and charming as she'd remembered, and oddly comforting in her distress.

Coming when it had, Eliza had latched desperately onto the invitation to relocate to New York. How she loved this glorious pale yellow cottage with its rounded turrets and abundance of gingerbread trim. It was one of a limited number of dwellings constructed of something other than brick or the varieties of stone so liberally used throughout the city. Inside and out, her aunt's loving touches lent rich beauty and homey grace wherever one's eye might fall. And here, far from Harrisburg, Eliza intended to put the past to rest and make a new start for herself.

Here she vowed to forget Weston Elliot and all his smooth words, the smiling lips that could bring all her dreams to life even as his cold heart could bring them dashing back to Earth again. She'd been a fool, so trusting, so naïve. But she wouldn't make that mistake in the future, not with a man—and *definitely* not with someone she considered a friend. Better to live and die friendless and a spinster than suffer such humiliation a second time.

Bitter anger at Melanie Brown had successfully repelled

that young woman's intrusion into Eliza's thoughts since she'd fled Harrisburg. But how would she ever banish her former betrothed from her mind when she'd be crossing paths with someone whose very appearance would be a constant reminder of the man who had stolen her untried heart and thoughtlessly smashed it into a million pieces?

two

Guiding his buggy away from Harper House, Micah gave his scarf an extra wrap about his neck. The storm had ended hours ago, and the last remnants of the clouds had long since moved out over the vast expanse of the Atlantic Ocean. The temperature, however, remained nippy even in the bright sunlight—especially with the breeze blowing across the ice-fringed Hudson River off to one side. Manhattan's close proximity to the sea both moderated and lessened the length of winter's cold snaps, so doubtless this one would dissipate soon enough.

Thinking of the funds provided by Mrs. Harper, he smiled to himself. The goodly sum would purchase a number of coats and mittens for the ragged orphans, plus some staple foods. The widow's giving spirit humbled Micah. For someone living alone for nigh unto a dozen years, she never once complained about her circumstances. She merely kept abreast of the needs of those less fortunate and did whatever she could to help out.

But his keen eye perceived that her health had been on the decline for some time now. How providential for God to send her a companion. Perhaps with extra hands and a caring person to look after her, the dear soul would gain new strength and find restored health. The world needed more folks as kindhearted as she.

Micah's recollections then drifted to her niece, whose delicate beauty seemed as appealing and fresh as Mrs. Harper's was creased with age. The young woman wore her sable hair parted in the middle with the back fashionably confined in a hair net, but tiny curls framing her face added a tangible softness. And despite the age difference between the two, Micah thought he'd ascertained a family resemblance in both features and carriage.

But there appeared no subtlety about Miss Eliza Criswell's reserve, he admitted. Her veiled eyes scarcely met his gaze long enough for him to identify their particular shade of blue. And in one unguarded moment he'd caught a glimpse of something that could only be termed anguish.

Well, no doubt she'd make some new friends once she began attending church services, and then perhaps her burdens would lighten. He would suggest to his fiancée, Anabelle, that she befriend Miss Criswell.

With that plan in mind, he snapped the reins sharply against the horse's back to pick up the pace.

❧

Eliza looked forward all week to the arrival of Sunday. Her spirit was in dire need of bolstering. Other times in her life when she'd faced disappointments and heartaches, she'd withdrawn from the Lord, becoming lax in her personal prayer and Bible reading. But that only led to more misery, more emptiness and hopelessness.

This time—perhaps from the utter shock of having been betrayed by two people she loved dearly—she turned to God for comfort and sanity, finding His grace sufficient, as the Bible promised. And here, far away from the pitying eyes of people who had known her all her life, she'd have the freedom to enter fully into the worship service.

To the casual observer, Faith Community Church definitely lacked the grandeur of the city's older and larger cathedrals. The steepled, red-brick building sported a new coat of pristine white paint around the windows, and the dormant shrubbery and trees flanking it were taller than Eliza remembered. Inside, however, its dark plank floor and walnut pews appeared much the same as they'd been years ago.

Relaxing beside Aunt Phoebe in the older woman's customary fourth row, she allowed her gaze to wander over the hushed sanctuary. There seemed to be very few people her own age, except for a slim, golden-haired organist playing a reverent prelude on the pump organ. Eliza focused on the young woman, noting the smoothness of her touch on the keys, the contrast between her fair complexion and the rich burgundy of her gown. With her every graceful move, muted colors from arched, stained-glass windows fell in a kaleidoscope of pastels over the wine velvet, accenting her lissome figure.

Eliza suddenly thought of Micah Richmond, remembering she hadn't seen him among the worshipers when she and her aunt made their way to their seats. Not that she was looking for him, especially, but his would have been the only other familiar face in this congregation of strangers.

Returning a few polite smiles from people around her, she shifted her attention forward.

Just then, the Reverend Thomas Norman rose from one of three large chairs on the platform and moved to the pulpit. He adjusted the sleeves of his charcoal suit as he surveyed his flock through gold-rimmed spectacles.

"I bid you all good morning on this lovely Lord's Day," he said, his smile warm and welcoming. "I'm certain Wilf Perkins has chosen some stirring hymns to lead off our service, but first, let us open with prayer." He bowed his graying head and spoke in a solemn voice. "Almighty God, Who sustains, guides, and protects us, we gather in Thy presence in humble thankfulness for Thy unfailing goodness and mercy to us all. Grant that we may worship Thee in spirit and in truth this day as we endeavor to glorify Thy Son, in whose name we pray. Amen."

Something about the pastor's manner greatly encouraged Eliza, and as the closing bars of the last hymn before the sermon faded and the man once again stepped to the lectern, she eagerly anticipated his words.

"Our text this morning is found in the fourth chapter of Philippians," he announced, "a passage with which I'm certain many of you dear folk are acquainted."

Eliza turned to it during the ensuing shuffle of crisp pages throughout the room.

"In this letter. . ." Pastor Norman's voice took on a booming quality, reverberating through the sanctuary. "The apostle Paul testified, 'I have learned in whatsoever state I am, therewith to be content.' And in writing to Timothy, upon another occasion, he proclaimed that 'godliness with contentment is great gain.' But how could someone who had suffered the magnitude of adversity which Paul endured ever find contentment in such troubled circumstances? That's what we are about to find out, dearly beloved, as we examine in depth the apostle's own words."

Eliza, musing over her own recent adversity, somehow gave the minister her whole attention while he continued relating the great saint's trials and suffering. She easily found the alternate passages used during the discourse. Many were already underlined in her Bible.

"But even a man as great as this," Pastor Norman continued, holding forth his large, frayed copy of the Scriptures, "was flesh and blood. He laughed, cried, got angry, became perplexed—and he was deeply conscious of his weaknesses. At times he openly acknowledged not only fear, but despair of life itself.

"Yet through it all, one thing held true. From his very conversion and subsequent trials, Paul was being drawn closer to the Lord, to His love and His power. He was being made like Him. Small wonder he could write, 'For to me to live is Christ, and to die is gain.' "

The words sounded oddly discomfiting to Eliza as she compared them to her own situation. Perhaps she hadn't shut herself off from God in this heartbreak, but she had yet to reach the point where she could forgive Weston for taking her love and throwing it back in her face. And Melanie's betrayal had seemed doubly cruel. Those wounds were still so fresh, the pain so intense. Eliza knew it would be a very long while before she could say in truth that she was becoming more like Christ—if ever. She needed to give the matter serious contemplation.

The minister paused and swept a glance around his congregation. "I'll close with this thought. The more satisfied we are with Jesus, the more we draw our strength from Him, the more firmly we'll stand up through all the bitter gales of adversity. Every believer can learn to find contentment in Him. It is, my friends, a matter of the heart. Let us pray. . . ."

Engrossed in her own thoughts, Eliza scarcely noticed as Mr. Perkins again took charge for the closing hymn and benediction.

Afterward, Aunt Phoebe took her hand and made the rounds, joyfully introducing her to the ladies of the church, a few deacons, and last of all, the pastor. But when her aunt became involved in a lengthy discussion with some friends from the Ladies' Benevolent Society, Eliza felt suddenly out of place. She meandered to the front of the sanctuary where the young woman in burgundy stood collecting her music.

"Excuse me," Eliza said tentatively.

The golden-haired girl turned, her gray-green eyes alight. "Yes?"

"I wanted to express to you how much I appreciated the music you played during the service."

"Why, thank you." A faint blush revealed a shy nature.

"I hate to admit it," Eliza continued, "but I was absolutely dreadful at my piano lessons, so I recognize a gift when I hear one."

The young woman smiled. "I'm Anabelle Dumont, and you're. . .?"

"Eliza Criswell, Phoebe Harper's niece, from Harrisburg."

"Oh, of course." An airy quality to her voice indicated a growing ease. "Micah told me about you. I believe you've already met him? Micah Richmond?" She scanned the departing crowd and frowned. "He was hoping to make the service this morning, but something else must have arisen."

"Yes, we've met," Eliza replied. "He came by my aunt's shop a few days ago."

"Well, I'm very pleased to meet you, Miss Criswell."

"Eliza. Please."

"Eliza then. And you must call me Anabelle. I assume we'll have many opportunities to get to know each other, now that you're living here in New York."

"I would imagine. Well, thank you—for the music, and for letting me bother you and all."

Anabelle blushed again. "It was no bother. Welcome to Faith Community. I hope you'll soon feel at home among us."

Eliza nodded and turned, rejoining her aunt, who was bidding the reverend good day. With a parting smile, she took the older woman's arm and assisted her down the steps to their waiting hired carriage.

"I see you met our fair Anabelle," Aunt Phoebe remarked as they plodded homeward. "She. . .keeps company, shall we say, with young Micah Richmond."

"Oh?" For some odd reason, Eliza's interest piqued, then flattened again in relief. Yet another reason she needn't waste thoughts on that particular man.

"Yes," her aunt went on. "Seems their families have enjoyed a close, lifelong relationship, so Ana and Micah have grown up together. Their parents naturally assume they'll wed one day."

"How nice." Eliza paused, choosing her next words with care. "I felt drawn to Anabelle, somehow. Her music, her. . . spirit. Something I can't name. Not that I'm seeking new friends, just now. But I couldn't help but notice there were very few young people in your church."

Her aunt's silver brows arched high. "Not seeking friends? Why, I've never heard of such a thing—especially since one couldn't find a sweeter companion than Anabelle Dumont.

Most of her peers have married and moved elsewhere, so I would imagine she would appreciate a new friend herself."

The mild rebuff made Eliza smile with chagrin.

"And you certainly don't need to be cloistered for days on end with no one but an old woman for company. I'll ask Ana over to tea," Aunt Phoebe determined. "I don't get out to many of the church functions or socials anymore, and I never go out at night in the winter. These old bones can't seem to take the cold the way they used to. But I'm sure she will manage a visit. I'll pass on the invitation through Micah when he stops by next."

Eliza gave a noncommittal nod and averted her attention to the passing scenery. This day, too, was clear and sunny, even though quite cold. Couples strolled arm in arm along the snowy path that ran alongside the Hudson River, happy and smiling as they exchanged adoring looks.

The reminder of her own loss brought a sharp jab of pain. Was her former fiancé even now parading his new *wife* along some wintry park setting for all the world to see? Anger rose up within her, stealing the pleasure of the day and, along with it, the joy she had derived from the music and the church service.

After reaching home and enjoying a light repast, Aunt Phoebe took advantage of the shop closure to lie down.

Eliza picked up the project she'd been working on and went upstairs to her room.

Cheery and bright, and looking out upon a broad expanse of the river several dozen yards away, the boudoir's entirely feminine decor displayed yet more of her aunt's artistry. It was papered beautifully with pale blue and white stripes on the lower portion and miniature roses above, and a hand-painted rose vine trailed above and below the white wainscoting. Eliza had spent a good part of her first day at her aunt's just admiring the perfectly rendered blooms.

Lowering herself onto the blue velvet chaise positioned to

take advantage of the window's light, she set to work again on the tatted border around the edge of a handkerchief. It would be some time before she would feel adroit at this delicate skill, but eventually she hoped to produce the quality of work someone might buy. Determined to master the art as quickly as possible, she worked carefully.

Mulling over the day's events and conversations brought to mind her new acquaintances. So Anabelle Dumont and Micah Richmond were keeping company, as Aunt Phoebe put it. It was easy enough to deduce what he saw in the organist, but what about the reverse? For the life of her, Eliza could think only of Weston when recollections of the child placement worker crossed her mind. And those thoughts were far from pleasant.

She frowned. She certainly wasn't being fair to the gentleman from Aunt Phoebe's church. After all, he'd been nothing but proper when they'd met. Perhaps she'd only imagined a resemblance between her former betrothed and this young man. Yes, that was it. She'd always been plagued by an overactive imagination, and in her present frame of mind, she might mistake anyone for the fiancé who had consumed all of her waking thoughts for the past few years.

Well, she certainly didn't need any reminders of Weston Elliot. She planned to erase him from her mind for good. She did not want to think about him—ever. For the rest of her life.

three

Ships and warehouses lined busy South Street along New York's East River, where piers stretched for a distance of three miles, in what was termed "Packet Row." The bustle of activity knew no season. Summer and winter, ocean vessels and packets of every size and purpose lay at anchor as passengers lined the quays and milled about, chattering to the small groups of individuals who had come to offer welcomes or bid farewells.

The area teemed with the clamor of street traffic, seabirds, and ships' whistles. Seamen of countless nationalities hollered to one another while hefting bulky ropes and moving cargo alternately aboard or ashore, according to their bills of lading. And not to be outdone, hawkers yelled above the melee, trying to entice customers to buy their wares.

Used to the confusion of the wharves, Micah paid it scarcely any mind as he hastened along, intent on his errand. A dockworker had informed him of a little homeless girl who'd been appearing out of nowhere whenever a new ship arrived. Belonging to no one, and with no other means to support herself, she would stand on the quay and sing, depending on some kind soul for a few pennies or dimes with which to buy her next meal.

This was not the first "singing girl" he'd heard of. The practice was heartbreakingly common among immigrant children orphaned by cholera or influenza. Such youngsters often sought meager shelter for the night in trash barrels or sometimes huddled against a closed door—anything to get out of the biting wind. Micah intended to find this little one a place to stay, even if only temporarily. Knowing the timid urchins feared the authorities, he kept a casual pace, his eyes darting about, searching likely hiding places.

At last he caught a movement on the edge of his vision. He turned his head slowly, feigning interest in some goods a passing peddler had for sale. Sure enough, he spied a street child. Painfully thin and ragged, bare-legged and hatless even in the bitter cold, she was scavenging in a refuse container. *Dear Father, she can't be more than seven or eight. And she needs help. Please give me wisdom in how to handle this situation.*

Experience taught him to go slowly in these instances. He took up a position behind an object that would prevent her from noticing him, then forced himself to stand by and do nothing except keep watch.

At that moment, the faraway blast from an incoming ship announced its approach.

Her head snapped in that direction, a tiny smile appearing in her dirty face as she meandered toward the available dock.

He smiled inwardly and followed. With her absorbed in performing for disembarking passengers, he just might manage to blend into the crowd. . .and have her sing for him. *Thank You, Father.*

It seemed to take an interminable amount of time for the vessel to chug its way into the harbor, drop anchor, and be secured. But at last Micah saw the gangplank lower into place. Passengers started down the wooden walkway.

As they neared the bottom, the little ragamuffin stepped out into plain view. Trembly at first, her thin, high voice broke forth in a hymn, gathering strength with each phrase.

Most folks completely ignored her.

Their callousness caught at Micah's heart. *Look at her!* he wanted to shout. *But for the grace of God, she could be your own little one!* But the new arrivals had more important things on their minds. Precious few tossed even a single coin in her direction.

Determined now, Micah merged into a group of descending folk and eased his way across to the other side of the gangplank, heading straight for the child.

"A song for ye, mister?" she asked shyly as he came nearer.

"Why, sure, young lady." He grinned, stopping to give her his whole attention. "Happen to know 'Abide with Me'?"

She nodded, her stringy hair bobbing with the motion. Opening her rosebud mouth, she sang the words perfectly, her grimy face shining with hope.

All the while he listened, Micah had to steel that portion of his heart that ached for each child such as this he encountered, willing the sorrow not to bring forth tears of anger, frustration, and grief.

"What do you suppose that song means?" he asked when she finished.

The thin shoulders beneath the threadbare coat shrugged.

"Do you know about God?"

Another shrug. "He lives up in heaven."

"Did you know He cares about you and wants to be your Friend?"

At this, her wary brown eyes took on a dubious look. "Are ye gonna give me money?"

Reaching into his coat pocket, Micah withdrew a pair of silver coins and dropped them into her tiny hand. When she appeared about to bolt, he dug for another. "Say, I was just about to go have something to eat. I don't suppose you're hungry?"

She stared for a moment before giving a grudging nod.

"Well, I know a place where there are lots of children, and they're just about to sit down to some hot soup and fresh bread. And after awhile, they'll be sleeping in warm, soft beds. Doesn't that sound nice?"

Her gaze dropped to the money in her palm, and she averted her eyes to the ground.

"And it doesn't cost one copper penny," Micah added

quickly. Watching the play of emotions in her face, he took a risk. "You know, honey, God happens to be a Friend of mine, and He told me you needed help. Would you let me help you? There's another snowstorm coming." His sober expression gave emphasis.

Until he said that, she remained passive. But then her eyes swam with tears.

It took every ounce of strength he possessed not to sweep her up into his arms. Instead, he offered a hand.

Turning her watery gaze to his, she hesitated briefly before placing her fingers into his palm.

Micah covered her tiny hand with his other one and smiled down at her. "My name is Micah. What's yours?"

"Rachel," she whispered, the gleam of hope in her eyes slowly overtaking the despair.

"My, but you're quiet this evening." Bringing a tray of tea and sliced nut bread into the parlor of her parents' home on fashionable Lexington Avenue, Anabelle set it on the coffee table before taking a seat beside Micah on the indigo brocade sofa. Matching gas lamps had been turned down low, and the soft, dim light gave the room an intimate air.

He smiled gently. "I had a rather long day."

"So I noticed," she said pointedly as the grandfather clock in the hall of the comfortable brownstone house chimed eight times. She poured each of them some of the rich amber liquid, handing one cup to him before helping herself to the other.

Micah reached for the cream pitcher and added a dollop as she stirred her usual two sugar cubes into hers. With the golden firelight as a backdrop, Anabelle's hair shone like a halo, and when she settled back against the sofa, her perfect profile appeared outlined in molten light. As always he admired her flawless, fragile beauty.

"What detained you?" she finally asked.

"I came across a street child this afternoon, one who needed food and a place to stay. It took awhile to arrange things."

"You were successful, then." Her words were more statement than question.

He nodded.

Anabelle sipped delicately from her cup, returning it to the saucer with an almost inaudible clink. "You know, Micah, I can't understand why you feel compelled to make all the city's orphans your personal responsibility."

He braced himself for the comments he knew would follow.

"There will always be needy children. Even the Bible says that. But here in New York the problem is almost overwhelming. You should be able to put in a day's work and then leave at a regular time, as does everyone else."

Her sentiments were not new. It seemed she'd said the same thing a thousand times before, in as many ways. Lacking energy to suppress his ragged sigh, he didn't fight it. "You know I feel called by the Lord to do what I do. It's not just a job; it's my ministry."

She gave a doubtful shrug. "I only know that the church provides considerable aid to the unfortunates through prayer and contributions and our benevolent activities. That should be enough."

"Well, it isn't enough, Ana. And it never will be. . .at least, not for me." Draining his tea, he set the cup onto the tray and started to rise.

Anabelle stopped him with a hand on his forearm. "Oh, please don't rush off, sweetheart. I haven't even had a chance to tell you I met Mrs. Harper's niece yesterday at service."

He sat back down. "Oh?"

"Yes. She seems ever so nice. Even lonely. . .perhaps because she's only recently arrived in the city."

"It's fortunate that her aunt will now have someone around to look after her. But by the same token, I'm sure Miss Criswell could use a friend, if you happen to be so inclined."

"I do, actually. We can always use extra hands on quilting days at church, and I'm thrilled at the prospect of having someone my age there. Those old biddies are forever talking to me as if I'm a schoolgirl."

He had to smile. "Well, at twenty-two, you're not all that far removed from being at Miss Witherspoon's Academy, you know."

Anabelle smiled dryly.

Micah brushed the curve of her fine cheekbone with his fingertips and gazed into her eyes—more gray than green in the subdued light. "Well, my dear, I am kind of tired. If you don't mind, I think I'll call it a night. Maybe tomorrow I'll be better company."

"Whatever you say." She took no offense from his early departure. "I'll make some taffy for when you come. Would you like that?"

"Sure. Sounds delicious." Rising, he pulled her lightly into his arms and gave her an equally soft kiss, attributing his own lack of passion to bone-weariness from his long day. "Take care, Ana. I'll see you tomorrow."

Sliding her arm about his waist, Anabelle rested her head against his shoulder and strolled with him to the door.

Outside once more in the cold night wind, Micah willed aside his nagging disappointment that the woman he planned to marry cared so little about what was most important to him. Perhaps that would change after they wed.

But what if it did not?

❧

Clothed in her warmest nightgown, Eliza stood at the mirror and removed her hair net and hairpins, allowing her long tresses to fall free of their usual confinement. She took the silver-handled brush her grandmother had given her years ago and began the habitual one hundred strokes.

Though this grand old mansion felt toasty during a sunny day, at night the wind's cold breath filtered through tiny cracks and crevices around the windows and along the floorboards. She hoped the warming pan had chased the chill from the bedsheets.

Finally reaching a hundred, Eliza set down the brush and padded to the fourposter. She removed the long-handled pan and climbed into the bed, arranging the fluffy quilts over herself before reaching for her Bible on the night table.

Pastor Norman's sermon still rang in her mind. And try as she might, she couldn't justify the ill feelings she still bore in her heart toward Weston—whom she blamed for everything, even Melanie's betrayal. After all, the girl had always been gullible to a fault. But determined to ease her own inner turmoil, Eliza read over the verses covered in the message, then clutched the Holy Book to her breast and bowed her head.

Dear Heavenly Father, I thank You for this lovely day and for Your presence even in our trials. I know that eventually I must let go of my anger and humiliation. . .and perhaps in time, I'll be able to do just that. But for now, I ask only that You stay close to me. Help me to remember that Your Son forgave even His murderers. Please don't let me forget His example. And if You can change my heart to be more like His, I am willing.

Even as that small admission came, Eliza realized she meant it and took that as an encouraging sign. She placed her Bible on the small table again and lay down with a sigh.

She loved being here with Aunt Phoebe. She hadn't particularly intended to seek out a new friend, yet it appeared the Lord was replacing Melanie with Anabelle Dumont. And Eliza was learning skills she had always coveted but somehow never found time to master.

Nevertheless, the future stretched before her, a bleak and empty road to nowhere. One she would travel alone, thanks to Weston Elliot. The wedding which she'd been planning for such a long time—and one which should have taken place by now—would never be.

She hoped her mother had returned all of the lovely gifts to which she was no longer entitled. And as for the pillowcases and other linens she'd so lovingly embroidered ever since girlhood for her married life, Eliza almost wished she had brought them along with her for the perverse pleasure of setting them ablaze!

No. On second thought, she'd sell them to help the needy. . . sell off her own chest of hopes, stop feeling sorry for herself, and find another purpose for her life just as her aunt had done.

But how, when she couldn't even find all the pieces of her shattered heart?

Hot tears she had long held back flooded her eyes, rolling down into her hair and onto her pillow. Eliza wept until she could weep no more.

four

"Utterly fascinating." Eliza peered over her aunt's shoulder at the exquisite lace collar being created by the aged fingers. Without missing a beat, Aunt Phoebe picked up a hand-carved bobbin from the myriad of wooden spools encircling her lace board. Then she wound the silk thread around and between the clusters of tiny pins positioned to form the intricate pattern she had designed. To Eliza, the finished portion appeared to be made of nothing but gossamer and air, and she felt reasonably certain she would never possess such skill.

"It's not really as difficult as it looks," her aunt said, "though it does require considerable practice."

"Indeed."

"My grandmother taught me when I was just a young girl. But with these old eyes, I dare not attempt it except on a bright morning like this. And that's one reason why I made this sunroom my work area."

"Still," Eliza marveled, "I wouldn't know where or how to start."

The white bun atop her aunt's head jiggled as she nodded, and she paused in her work to meet Eliza's gaze. "Making lace always reminds me of life," she began thoughtfully. "We're the pins on the board, and God is the great Weaver. He picks up a thread from some faraway corner and winds it around us. We might not feel a particular strand is so very comfortable as He first pulls it taut. But there's no point in struggling against it. From His viewpoint, He's fashioning a design that brings glory to every aspect of His handiwork. And one day, when we look back on our lives, we'll see things of beauty even in the places we thought were dark and hard."

The lovely sentiments touched Eliza, and she mused over them momentarily before focusing again on her own task. "Well, I'll be satisfied if I can master tatting." With a critical grimace, she sank back into her chair in the workroom and held her own project at arm's length to assess her stitches.

"I wouldn't fret overmuch," Aunt Phoebe said kindly. "From what I've seen of your labors so far, I'd say those handkerchiefs will not remain in the shop very long before someone buys them."

As if on cue, the bell above the parlor door reverberated through the hall, signaling the arrival of a customer.

The older woman stood. "I'll tend to this one."

"And I'll see about dinner. It's nearly noon." Laying her task aside, Eliza rose and headed for the kitchen. But she couldn't dismiss the mental picture her aunt had painted. Could being rejected and cast aside like some unwanted, disdainful object ever be part of her own life's beautiful pattern? She had her doubts. No matter how she attempted to distance herself from her circumstances, they would forever appear cruel and ugly.

In the kitchen, Eliza opened the icebox, removed a pair of eggs and set them to coddling, then sliced two thick chunks of bread to toast and butter. Small dishes of canned peaches with sweetened cream, ladyfingers, and a pot of tea topped off the light midday meal. Putting all the items on a large tray, she carried them to the parlor.

Her aunt, she discovered upon her approach, had not as yet finished with the customer. Not wanting to intrude, Eliza hesitated before entering the room.

"As always, we can only do our best," came Micah Richmond's familiar voice. "Things are going from bad to worse as winter settles in. Conditions at the tenements are deplorable beyond words, as you know."

"Yes, and it's such a pity," her aunt replied. "Let us pray that the good ladies at Faith Community will be able to step up their provisions in the weeks to come. I've been saving material scraps left over from some of my own projects. I'll add them to the quilt supplies at the church."

"I'm sure that'll be much appreciated. You are a good friend."

Eliza surmised from the tone of the conversation that the young man was about to depart. She waited for the sound of the door. When it didn't come directly, she sighed and propped the heavy serving tray against a hip.

With her movement, a teaspoon fell over the edge and clattered noisily to the floor.

"Is that you, Eliza, dear?" Aunt Phoebe called out.

Eliza knew it would be pointless—and rude—not to respond. "Yes." Forcing a smile, she gripped her burden more firmly and stepped into the room, heading for the nearest table.

"Ah, Miss Criswell." The young man gave a slight bow of his head as she moved into view. "Good day."

"And a good day to you, Mr. Richmond." Eliza had all but convinced herself she had only imagined the resemblance between the man and her former fiancé, but to her dismay, the merest glance proved the opposite to be true. She caught her breath at the amazing similarities and purposely refrained from meeting his gaze as she turned away and put all her efforts into setting a proper table.

"Oh, that reminds me, Micah," her aunt said, "Eliza and I would love for Anabelle to come to tea. Tomorrow afternoon, if it's convenient. Would you be kind enough to deliver this note to her?"

"Delighted to be of service, Mrs. Harper. It's not often I get to do something in return for your kindnesses. I shall take my leave so you ladies can enjoy your meal." Plunking his hat on, he tipped his head politely and exited with a carefree wave of the hand.

Last week's snow had melted days ago, and the sound of

his footfalls drifted from the front walk as he strode out to his carriage.

"Such a nice, nice young man," Aunt Phoebe said, coming to take a seat at the table. "Oh, this looks lovely, dear."

❧

A fairly steady stream of patrons, mindful of the approaching Christmas season, came to the shop the next morning. Aunt Phoebe had assigned kitchen duty to Eliza, and Eliza suspected that her aunt hoped the chore of providing an array of freshly baked treats for afternoon tea would help occupy her until their guest arrived. But she wondered if her aunt felt more nervous than she did. From bits of conversation, Eliza guessed that Aunt Phoebe didn't want her niece being cut off with other young people simply because she was living with an older woman. With the exception of Micah's brief visits, the afternoon tea with Anabelle would be the first time they had entertained someone Eliza's age since she'd moved from Harrisburg.

Finally four o'clock arrived, and with it, the carriage bringing Anabelle. Aunt Phoebe ushered the fair-haired beauty inside and turned the *Closed* sign outward.

"Lovely to see you both again," Anabelle said airily as she hung her fur-lined wrap on the hall tree beside the door and tucked her long gloves into its roomy hood. Her cheeks glowed pink from the brisk temperature, a fitting contrast to the rich emerald gown she wore. Its sleeves fairly dripped with rich ecru lace every bit as delicate as her soft skin.

"We're so pleased you could come," Eliza answered, thankful that she'd taken the time to change into a dressier frock after the day's baking was finished.

"Why don't we all be seated?" Aunt Phoebe motioned to the lace-draped table, and the three of them took chairs.

Eliza felt her face flush with pride when Anabelle glanced appreciatively at the assortment of fancy cookies, fudge, and teacakes she had labored over most of the day. She had done her best to prepare something that Anabelle would enjoy, and she sighed with thankfulness that everything had turned out perfectly.

Aunt Phoebe offered a brief prayer over the food, and then filled the floral-patterned teacups.

"Everything is just exquisite," Anabelle said, her tone completely sincere. "I've often envied your talents, Mrs. Harper." Scooping two sweet cubes from the silver sugar scuttle, she stirred them into her tea before taking a sip.

Aunt Phoebe smiled. "If you're referring to the array of gifts about the room, I am happy to announce that my niece is acquiring some splendid proficiency along those lines already. If you're speaking of our refreshments, however, I must confess they are all Eliza's doing."

"You don't say." Anabelle turned a gracious smile on Eliza. "Well, music might come easily to me, Eliza, but I'm afraid my accomplishments in the kitchen lag far behind yours."

"Thank you," she replied demurely.

"Speaking of music," Aunt Phoebe chimed in, "we'd love it if you would favor us with a piece when we've finished eating. Something from the classics, perhaps."

"As you wish." Sampling one of the dainty cookies on her plate, Anabelle switched her attention to Eliza once more. "Are you enjoying your stay in New York?"

"Very much. I've been quite busy and have met many friendly folk at the church and here at our shop. Of course, Auntie always makes me feel at home whenever I come to visit."

The honey-blond nodded in agreement. "All of us at Faith Community have basked in her hospitality on occasion. I'm pleased to hear you're fitting in so well. In fact, it would be a boon to the sewing circle if you would consider joining us on Thursday afternoons. At present, we're working on quilts for the unfortunates. Micah delivers them where they're most needed."

"Why, I'd be delighted to help out, if Aunt Phoebe can spare me for a few hours each week." She flashed a questioning glance at her aunt, who nodded.

"Wonderful!" Anabelle exclaimed. "I'll have my driver come by for you on Thursdays at one o'clock." She laughed lightly. "At last, someone near my own age! You cannot imagine what it's like to be among ladies who treat me as if I'm still in pigtails."

With a pointed look at the two of them, Aunt Phoebe finished the last of her tea and got up. "I hope you'll both excuse me if I leave you two *youngsters* to visit while I do a bit of dusting and rearranging of goods on the store shelves."

"Not at all," they both answered.

Anabelle bit into a piece of fudge as the older woman left the room. When she spoke again, her tone was soft, almost conspiratorial. "I know quite a number of eligible bachelors who might enjoy your company also, Eliza. I'd be happy to introduce you around. Perhaps Micah and I could escort you and—"

Eliza blanched. "Thank you, but no. I'm not at all interested in that sort of thing."

"Oh." Her color heightening, Anabelle readjusted her napkin. "What a pity. Well, all the same, I shall be glad for your company at the sewing circle."

Sensing her guest's discomfort, Eliza decided to change the subject. "So, what other interests do you have that occupy your time beside music and needlework?"

The slender blond relaxed noticeably. "I'm an avid reader, absolutely devouring whatever new fiction comes into the bookseller's. And, of course," she added on a note of chagrin, "my mother insists I prepare supper at least twice every week. She's bound and determined to marry me off to Micah at the earliest opportunity."

The constant references to the young woman's beau were oddly comforting to Eliza, instilling in her a deeper conviction that she need not be ill at ease in his presence. After all, he wasn't Weston; he had no designs on her. And she truly did want to become friends with Anabelle. Seeing that the girl seemed to have finished eating, Eliza folded her own napkin. "Shall I show you to the piano now?"

"Oh, yes. I'm sure that my fingers have finally thawed sufficiently."

Half an hour and a dozen etudes later, Eliza felt completely at ease with Anabelle Dumont. "I shall never cease coveting your talent," she finally admitted. Resting against her aunt's ebony satin upright, she watched the girl's nimble fingers caressing the ivory keys. "When I think of how I detested all those dreary scales and tiresome arpeggios, it's no wonder I drove many a music tutor mad."

Anabelle's laugh sounded as fittingly musical as her ability. "And I, on the other hand, could not get enough of playing. My mother often threatened to put a leash around my neck so she could drag me away from the piano for meals."

At this, Eliza sputtered into a giggle, and Anabelle nearly doubled over with mirth.

"Now that's what's been missing from this old house," Aunt Phoebe murmured, coming into the room. "The sound of music and youth and laughter."

"I've just been trying to absorb a measure of Anabelle's gift," Eliza said, gathering her composure again. "It reminds me how foolish it is to waste one's opportunities in life."

"So what is it you desire?" her new friend asked. "A second chance?"

"Are you offering to teach me?" Eliza, only half jesting, sobered. "Because, if you're serious, I think I truly would like to study the piano again. I'm older now. The thought of scales and practice aren't nearly so unbearable as they seemed in my girlhood."

"Agreed." Anabelle crossed her arms and gave a decisive nod. "We'll do it on Fridays then. That is, assuming my coming here won't upset your schedule, Mrs. Harper." She swept a glance up to the older woman, who at this point appeared to be in shock.

With a shake of her snowy head, she recovered nicely. "No, no. Whatever you two decide is fine with me. I'll still have Eliza to help me the rest of the time."

But when Eliza searched her aunt's lined face, she saw something she hadn't been aware of before. . .a deep love for her. Concern for her welfare. She couldn't resist the urge to hug the kind woman.

As she did, the future which had seemed to hold nothing but bleakness and despair such a short time ago shone with brighter facets. She may not have become the new bride she had expected to be—and possibly never would—but the Lord held her life in His hands. And for the most fleeting of seconds, Eliza could almost glimpse a measure of beauty taking shape in the pattern He'd chosen.

five

The smartly fitted black and red barouche rolled smoothly behind matched chestnut geldings. Despite Eliza's best intentions to put her unhappiness behind her, the grayness of the afternoon sky cast a pallor over her spirit as she rode with her new friend to the quilting circle meeting.

"You'll just love the dear ladies who come every week to sew," Anabelle gushed. "Especially the Madison sisters, Francine and Frederica. Sadly enough, they nursed their sickly parents for so many years, life has passed them by. But a kinder, more selfless pair of spinsters you'll never find, to say nothing of their blithesome natures. They inspire the rest of us to accept whatever befalls."

Eliza stifled a grim smile, wondering if one day someone would make a similar comment about her. *Poor Eliza Criswell. For an old maid, she remains amazingly cheerful. I hear she came near to marrying at one time, but her beau ran off with her best friend. Tsk, tsk.*

"It's to be commended, don't you think?"

Realizing Anabelle was awaiting her response, Eliza felt a flush crest her face. "Forgive me; I was thinking about something else and missed what you said."

"No matter," Anabelle said, her fair complexion a stark contrast against the coat's deep blue hood. "I get rather carried away at times with my chattering. It's one of my worst faults. I didn't mean to bore you."

"Oh, you weren't boring me. Not at all. Please, do continue with what you were saying."

As if to make sure the plea was sincere, Anabelle scrutinized her for a few seconds, then picked up the thread of conversation. "I was merely stating that Faith Community Church provides many kinds of aid to the immigrants, and thanks to the efforts of the Madison sisters, many other city churches have now undertaken similar programs."

"Yes, that is splendid. From what I've heard, the need is great."

"Quite true. I confess, however, that I fail to share Micah's obsession for the unfortunates. How he can set foot in those horrid, smelly places, I'll never know. But after all, some of us labor best from behind the lines."

"I heartily agree."

At this, a broad smile lit Anabelle's blithe countenance. "I knew it. From the moment we met, I've had a most profound conviction that we're kindred spirits."

"So did I!" Eliza returned the smile. "I'm glad we've become friends."

The carriage slowed upon nearing the neat, steepled church, then drew to a stop.

Anabelle pushed aside the fur lap robe covering their legs as the lanky, black-coated driver hopped down from his seat.

"I'll call back for you at half-past three, miss," he said pleasantly, lifting his prominent chin when he helped Anabelle and Eliza alight from the conveyance.

"Thank you, Graham; that will be fine. Come, Eliza." Gathering her skirt in one hand on her way up the church steps, Anabelle waited at the top landing for Eliza, and together they entered the building. "We use the basement for our work, since it's near the furnace and therefore the quickest to heat."

Once inside, they hung up their outer wraps and immediately took the stairwell off to the right. Quiet voices from below floated up to meet them, growing louder on their descent.

When they emerged into the open, Eliza saw that long worktables had been pushed end-to-end, dominating the center of the large room, their flat surfaces sporting piles of assorted materials and works in progress. A dozen or more seamstresses lined both sides.

"Good day, ladies," Anabelle sing-songed.

The workers turned their heads, light glinting off an array of eyeglasses perched on the various noses.

Eliza manufactured a brave smile.

"I've brought a newcomer to join us," Anabelle went on. "I'm sure many of you met Eliza Criswell this past Sunday at service. She lives at Harper House now and will be helping with our projects."

"Splendid," a frail waif of an elderly woman said, her voice crackling. "The more the merrier."

"Yes, we're thrilled to have additional hands," a second, plumper matron added.

Recognizing a number of faces as Anabelle rattled off everyone's names, Eliza released a small breath of relief. She wasn't going to feel so much like a stranger here after all.

"And you must get to know this charming duo." Anabelle moved to drape her arms about the shoulders of two bony but handsome ladies of advanced years. "These are the Madison sisters, Miss Francine and Miss Frederica, our mainstays here at Faith Community."

"So good to make your acquaintance," the more outspoken of the two said, while her sister gave a beaming nod. "You girls make yourself right at home." She waved a spindly, blue-veined hand in the direction of an available spot where they could sit together.

Anabelle perused the multicolored quilt draping the work space between the sisters. "Oh, I see you've nearly finished that one. Eliza and I will begin piecing a new top." She helped herself to the scissors, needles, and thread they would need, then rooted through the available scraps, which she placed in close proximity for working.

The afternoon went swiftly for Eliza, listening to the chatter and gentle teasing passing back and forth among the workers, but she couldn't help wondering how Aunt Phoebe was making out on her own.

Idly surveying the work going on around her, she noticed a lovely finished coverlet similar to one her mother had pieced years ago for a hope chest better forgotten. Before the memory could inflict pain, she centered on the need to write home and let her parents know that being here in New York agreed with her.

As the session wound down to a close and two ladies folded a newly finished quilt, the heavy clomp of masculine footsteps sounded from the stairs. Micah Richmond entered, his face red from the outside chill. "Greetings, ladies. Thought I'd come by for the latest offerings." He rubbed his gloved hands together as if to generate some warmth.

"We've done three more this afternoon," one of the Madisons informed him. "Now that we've got a new helper—" She smiled at Eliza graciously. "We should be a little more productive each month."

"Wonderful." He grinned at the older woman before turning his deep-set hazel eyes upon Eliza. "I assure you, we can use as many of these as your nimble fingers can provide."

Eliza watched Anabelle move to his side, the young woman's gaze and her smile dreamy as they rested on his manly features. When Micah drew her within the crook of his arm, the sight sent a sad remembrance through Eliza. She lowered her lashes and busied herself helping the others set the work area to rights once more.

Micah would have had to be blind not to notice the bright spots of color both Anabelle and Eliza provided amid this gathering of somberly attired matrons and widows. Not only had the pair dressed in rich jewel hues, but they were the only two whose hair was neither white nor some shade of gray. Even their faces bore a youthful radiance, with Miss Criswell's taking on a deeper rose whenever he looked her way. Curious, how she never quite met his eyes, but perhaps she was shy.

"Well, now," he said casually, tightening his arm about Anabelle's slender form, "I know some folks who will truly appreciate your tireless labors. I thank you from the bottom of my heart. We'll waste no time in delivering them where they're most needed."

"Will I see you this evening?" Anabelle asked as he released her and moved away to pick up the neat stack of quilts waiting at the end of one table.

"Most likely."

"Marvelous. We'll expect you for supper then."

"Fine. I'll be there." Leaning to plant a quick peck on her cheek, he gave her chin a loving tweak with his free hand, then waved good-bye to the others. "Thanks again, ladies. God bless you all."

Mounting the stairs two at a time, he hurried to his waiting buggy. He'd head directly to Child Placement to collect his assistant, Mrs. Wallace, and the two of them would take the coverlets to some needy tenement families. And after that, he'd go to Ana's.

Thoughts of his intended rambled through his busy mind, and he smiled. She seemed much happier since Eliza Criswell's arrival in town. The pair seemed to get along royally, which was gratifying, considering he'd suggested Anabelle befriend Mrs. Harper's niece mainly for the newcomer's benefit. But whatever the outcome of this blossoming friendship, he appreciated seeing those green eyes of Anabelle's sparkling again.

He only wished he had generated some of that dazzle himself.

❧

When Eliza got home, she found her aunt in her favorite rocking chair, working on a needlepoint case for spectacles.

The older woman looked up. "Did you enjoy your outing, my dear?"

"Oh, yes. It's rather amazing to see how much a group of

women can accomplish in a single afternoon. And it's a joy to be with Anabelle." She drew a hesitant breath. "Her beau stopped by when we were finishing up."

"Is that so?" Aunt Phoebe nudged her special sewing glasses a notch higher but continued to peer over them at her.

"Yes, to pick up the finished quilts." Even as she elaborated on Micah Richmond's visit, Eliza wondered why she'd bothered to mention it. Nevertheless, she could not restrain her tongue. "It seems he delivers them almost the moment the last thread has been tied."

"That does not surprise me. I've yet to meet a more industrious lad. His parents would have been proud of his generous spirit. Of course, to be truthful, he is much like they were themselves. It was a great loss to our church when his dear mother passed away suddenly, to be followed soon after by his father. Of course, Micah's family and Anabelle's were very close friends, and the Dumonts treat him like their own son. He will be, soon enough, I expect."

Eliza nodded thoughtfully, reflecting on the striking couple Anabelle and Micah made.

The older woman studied her for a moment. "It does my heart good to see you perking up, dear. I don't mind telling you, I was quite concerned over you when you first arrived from Harrisburg."

"I suppose I'm destined to live after all," Eliza admitted candidly, then paused with a sad smile. "But still, there are certain things I can't allow myself to dwell on just yet."

Her aunt nodded. "I never met that young man of yours, so I realize I'm making a rash judgment when I speak ill of him. But I've known you all your life, Eliza, and it boggles this old mind that anyone could treat you shamefully."

With suppressed tears so very near the surface these days, Eliza fought hard to keep them at bay.

"But never you mind about him, my dear. It has always been my experience that the Lord never takes something away from us without replacing it with something better. And I'm sure He has someone wonderful and more deserving of you in store. Wait and see." She picked up her needlepoint and resumed working.

Watching her, Eliza pondered those last statements. She sincerely doubted she wanted to be that vulnerable again—ever. Just now that was about the last thing on her list of desires. But considering her aunt's optimistic statement, Eliza felt the need to clarify it. "Auntie, when the Lord took Uncle Amos all those years ago, did He send you someone. . .better?"

The old hands stilled once more, and the watery blue eyes turned to her. "Yes and no. Of course, I could never imagine loving another man the way I did my Captain. It was like losing a part of myself when his ship went down. Took me ages to stop looking out the window, expecting to see him coming up the walk with those long sweeping strides of his, hearing that jaunty whistle that so cheered my days."

A wistful expression gentled the creases in the aged countenance. "But gradually I became aware of the soothing presence of the Comforter Whom God tells us about in His Word. The Holy Spirit became very real to me, in a way I'd never experienced before. And He is a great blessing and has been through the years. That is what has sustained me since Cap's been gone."

Eliza felt the gathering tears trembling on her lashes. Her heart ached for Aunt Phoebe's loss and for her own. Perhaps the day would come when she could think of Weston and Melanie without wanting to scream or cry. But at the moment she felt compelled to go and hug her aunt, perhaps absorb some of that peaceful spirit that somehow radiated from her very being.

Tonight, she would ask God to make His presence more real in her own empty life. Anything to fill the aching void that gaped within her heart.

six

Thanksgiving, a quiet affair for two, provided a time of challenge, with Eliza and her Aunt Phoebe trying to outdo one another in relating their blessings. Though it started out in all seriousness over dried apple pie after a small but delectable feast, it soon became apparent that neither wanted to relinquish the opportunity to have the last word.

"Well, I am thankful to still be living here at Harper House," the older woman said, "where so many of life's precious memories still bring me joy."

Eliza tipped her head respectfully. "And I am glad you're still here, making precious memories with me."

"How sweet. And now that you mention it, I am thankful to have company at last. To hear someone else's footsteps and laughter besides my own."

"Then, both of us are grateful to Weston for furnishing me with a reason to come!" Even though Eliza had spoken without thinking, the fact that she truly meant it made her sputter into a giggle. Her aunt joined in, and they laughed until tears ran down their faces.

For a brief moment, Eliza feared she would not be able to stop crying, and the astute older woman's expression gentled.

"It hurt very deeply, I would expect."

Eliza blotted the corners of her eyes on her napkin and nodded. "Perhaps it might have been easier to bear if—" She could hardly utter the words. "Why did he have to choose my very dearest friend?" Tears again blurred her vision, and she rushed to say the rest before her throat closed up. "I could have turned to Melanie for solace, but instead, I've had to learn to live without her, too."

"I know, child." Aunt Phoebe inhaled slowly, deeply. Her loving fingers stroked Eliza's arm, letting her cry as long as she needed to. "Sometimes I wonder how we manage to endure some of the losses we are asked to suffer. And all I can say is that our heavenly Father's heart breaks right along with ours, and then He gives the strength we need."

When Eliza's inner turmoil subsided, she gathered herself together. She searched the kind, frail face across the table, and her heart swelled with love. "You know, Auntie, not too long ago, I wondered if I would ever be happy again. But somehow, since coming to be with you, I've actually started 'forgetting the past,' as the apostle Paul put it. Not that I have come up with any grandiose plans for my future, mind you. I don't care to look that far ahead. But at least I can trust God for today without fearing what tomorrow may bring. Does that sound strange?"

"Not at all, my dear, not at all." Closing her crooked fingers over Eliza's, she smiled. "I would say it's an answer to prayer." Her blue eyes sparkled again. "For which I am deeply grateful."

"Oh, no!" Eliza laughed in feigned shock. "Now you've made it my turn again. . . ."

❧

November ended and December took its place, bringing shorter, changeable days which featured brilliant sunshine or banks of endless gray clouds. Holly boughs and evergreen wreaths tied with crimson ribbons lent a festive air to lamp-posts and front doors all over the city.

In view of the coming holidays, Aunt Phoebe set out an abundance of red candles and velvet-bowed decorations. And the bell above the gift shop door rang with more frequency, necessitating long evenings of labor to replace merchandise which had been sold.

Eliza took pride in the quality of work she now turned out, both at home and in the quilting circle at church. But most of all, she treasured her times of solitude in her room when she sought the company of the loving Comforter Whose soothing presence her aunt so appreciated. Morning and evening Bible reading and prayer became less a duty and more a joyous communion with a dearest Friend. And in the light of the indescribable peace that now filled Eliza, past disappointments faded into insignificance as she began to pray that her life would have meaning and purpose.

On Thursday, Anabelle stayed home in bed with a cold but sent her driver as usual to transport Eliza to church. While she was glad to go, Eliza found the activity rather lonely without the willowy young woman's company and good-natured chatter. Nevertheless, the afternoon did pass swiftly, with four more coverlets completed.

It was Eliza's turn to tidy up at the close of the sewing session, so after the other ladies put away the supplies and took their leave, Eliza swept the loose threads from the floor. The silence of the almost-empty building magnified the peculiar creaks and groans caused by the wind, sounds that had been scarcely noticeable earlier amid the banter and conversation. Now they echoed hollowly from wall to wall. Eager to be finished with the chore, she hurriedly dumped the dustpan into a waste bin in the storage closet.

A door opened upstairs. Eliza assumed Anabelle's driver had come for her.

But the heavy footsteps that clambered down to the basement brought Micah Richmond instead, his shoulders sporting a dusting of snowflakes. "Where is everyone?" he asked jovially.

Eliza smiled, his sudden appearances no longer catching her off guard. "You just missed them. They went home not five minutes ago."

"And left you with the drudgery, I see," he teased.

"We take turns, actually."

"Ah." He scanned the room. "Ana's not here?"

"Sorry, no. She's under the weather this afternoon."

"Oh, yes. She complained of a chill last evening, as I recall. I'll run by later and look in on her."

Eliza nodded and gathered her belongings together.

"I assume these are today's completed quilts?" He tipped his head toward the end of the table.

"Yes. Four this time."

"Wonderful." Micah picked them up and took a few steps toward the doorway, then turned. "Uh, Miss Criswell? I don't suppose—"

"What is it?"

"Must you go home directly?"

Her eyes widened. "Well, naturally Aunt Phoebe expects me soon after the close of the quilting circle. I did tell her and Anabelle's driver that I would be detained a few minutes after the session. But Graham might be waiting for me." Noticing Micah's troubled expression, she paused. "Why do you ask?"

"It's nothing. Never mind." Filling his lungs, he started away, but halted again. "On second thought, I might as well come out with it. I'm in dire need of a favor."

"I beg your pardon?"

A sheepish grin appeared on his lips. "I was hoping to deliver these right away, but my assistant was called out of town to her daughter's home on an emergency. I was wondering if you could possibly accompany me."

Eliza merely stared, unsure how to respond.

"Many women at the tenements have been widowed or deserted by their husbands," he explained, "and they're more at ease if I bring a female companion along. I promise not to keep you a moment longer than absolutely necessary."

"I–I don't know what to say."

He released a disappointed breath. "I understand. It was just a thought. Sorry to impose on you."

His deflated expression tugged at her heart and made her

change her mind. She'd probably regret doing so later, but after all, he wasn't asking that much of her. "Wait!"

He halted on the steps and looked back.

"If you're sure it would help, I suppose it couldn't hurt for me to go along this once."

Micah's strong, manly features took on a boyish quality with his grin. "Splendid. I'll not keep you long, I assure you."

But even as Eliza followed him up the stairwell, she wondered if her decision had been a rash one. Hadn't Anabelle told her he often went to disreputable areas of town?

Outside, the Dumonts' coach indeed stood waiting. Micah went to thank the driver for his trouble and sent him on his way. Then he assisted Eliza into his much plainer buggy, climbed aboard himself, and took the reins. "I truly appreciate your willingness to help me out, Miss Criswell."

He clucked the horse forward, guiding it out among the assortment of other conveyances on the busy street. "Would you think me terribly forward if I were to call you Eliza? Since you're such a good friend of Ana's, and she speaks of you so often, I thought perhaps you'd consider me a friend as well."

The brief recollection of the last man who called her by her first name brought a pang, but Eliza ignored it. "As you wish." Her breath crystallizing in the cold air, she tucked her hands into the fur muff which complemented her winter coat. Soft feathery snowflakes swirled around them.

"Then you must call me Micah. It will save time, not to mention be less cumbersome."

She gave a perfunctory nod and averted her attention to the passing residences on either side of the unfamiliar Manhattan thoroughfare as the horse's hooves clopped in regular cadence over the pavement. Stately and well-tended, the grand homes had lovely grounds whose summer glory could only be imagined. But even beneath winter's cold spell their subdued beauty was a sight to behold as the profusion of old trees reached lacy crowns toward the heavens.

Micah didn't seem very talkative, and Eliza sensed he had a lot on his mind. Without the need for polite conversation, she concentrated on the sights that were completely new to her as the buggy turned onto Broadway. There her gaze drank in the limitless variety of stores and tall buildings whose tops scraped the sky. Signs of the approaching holiday season abounded in colorful window displays of the latest in fashion and children's toys.

When they passed city hall and neared the East River, however, the scenery took a turn for the worse. The streets became narrower and more crooked. Dwellings looked gloomy and wretched and crowded together. And despite the salt-laden breeze coming from the vast Atlantic, whose briny waters mingled with that of many of the large rivers along the eastern coastline, a foul stench from the refuse-filled gutters pervaded the air.

Eliza surveyed the conglomeration of grim, multistory dwellings in Manhattan's lower East Side. In various stages of disrepair, all of them fairly teemed with inhabitants. She was appalled at the cheerless appearance of the tenements, to say nothing of the hordes of hopeless-looking people and ragged children seemingly everywhere. Dismal, frozen clothing and diapers flapped from clotheslines strung high above the narrow road from windows opposite each other, and Eliza couldn't begin to discern the number of foreign languages being bandied about.

"I can't believe people live like this." Having actually uttered that thought aloud, she cringed with embarrassment.

"You haven't seen anything yet." Drawing the horse to a halt midway down one of the cobbled lanes, Micah got out and helped her down, then reached for the quilts. "Just stay close to me."

He needn't have said it. Nothing would have made Eliza venture anywhere by herself.

As bad as the exteriors of the tenements looked, the interiors proved even worse. In her wildest imaginings she wouldn't have dreamed such filth existed, or that people could actually spend their days in such horrid conditions. Clutching her skirt to keep the hem out of the grime, she doggedly followed Micah into the common hall of one of the buildings, their footsteps echoing off the cracked plaster walls and bare floors. A rickety staircase, out of reach of the faint light struggling to penetrate the single window at the other end of long corridor, ascended into utter darkness.

"Mr. Micah! Mr. Micah!" The gleeful, boyish voice carried the entire length of the dreary hall. The patter of little feet followed immediately as a curly-headed boy sprang up from where he'd been sitting in an open doorway and flew to throw his arms around Micah's legs. His shirt gaped where a button was missing, and his trousers were too short, but his exuberant greeting lacked nothing at all.

"Hi there, Vinnie." Micah knelt to return the hug, the bulky quilts clutched in the crook of one arm. "What's up, buddy?"

By now, other little ones peeked out into the hall from the same room as well as other rooms lining the hallway. They all came running.

Eliza stood back in amazement, watching her companion tousle hair, hug shoulders, and pat heads in turn. The sight warmed her heart, and she returned each timid glance with a smile she hoped appeared friendly.

"Guess'a what, Mr. Micah?" a scraggly-haired girl of about five said in a conspiratorial tone. She toyed with the torn pocket of her faded dress. "Rosa and Gabriella's mama, she gone'a to da angels. Dey both'a stay'a wit us."

His cheery expression turned somber. "I thought she was getting better." Then he gave a nod of resignation. "Well, I'm on my way to see your mother right now. Come on, Gina. Think you can show my friend, Miss Eliza, the way?"

The little one gave Eliza a dubious glance, but with a sigh, took her hand. "Dis'a way."

Trying not to reveal her dismay at the grubby little fingers and dirt-smudged face, Eliza allowed herself to be led along.

Two doors farther down, Micah rapped on the jamb. "Mrs. Garibaldi?"

The youngsters clustered around him, their huge brown eyes adoring as they stroked the fine material of his winter coat.

"Eh? Who'sa dere?" came a voice from inside. Seconds later, wiping her hands on the soiled apron covering her threadbare cotton dress, a large-boned, frazzled woman of indeterminate age appeared. "Oh. Mr. Richmond. Come in'a, come in." She eyed the bounty he carried, then glared pointedly at the children. "Hey, bambinos. Whatsa matta you bother da nice'a man, eh? Go. Play." Waving them away, she leaned out the door to watch them go down the hall.

Micah peeled off the top quilt. "This is for you. You said last time that you could use another one."

"*Graci.* Vittorio and'a me, we appreciate dis."

While Micah talked to the lady of the house, Eliza couldn't help looking around the bleak, narrow room in the feeble glow from a kerosene lamp. She could smell the stew simmering in a pot on the stove at the far end. Worn, sparse furnishings in no particular arrangement filled most of the wall space. Her heart went out to the young, curly-haired baby sitting on a blanket remnant on the otherwise bare floor, sucking on the sole of an old shoe. Surprisingly, though cramped and cheerless, the place seemed somewhat tidy, even if far from clean.

"Gina told me Mrs. Riccio passed on. Is that true?" Micah asked.

"*Si.* Yesterday, noon. Dey already take'a da remains. Vittorio say to me, 'Sophia,' he say, 'Giuseppe and Anna Marie our friends'a since Naples, eh? We should keep'a

Rosa and Gabriella for our friends.' So, bambinos, dey stay wit us, like'a before. Where else dey go?"

Micah gave a noncommittal shrug. "Won't they be a bother with your own children to look after, your sewing, and all?"

"What else friends'a do, eh? Dey live here when'a we all come to America. Dey play wit our Maria an' Gina, you know?"

"Well, if they get to be a burden, tell me. I might be able to find a place for them."

She nodded, albeit reluctantly.

"Where are the girls now?" Micah asked.

"Asleep. Dey cry an' cry. Dey finally sleep."

"Mind if we look in on them?"

Just then the baby toppled over and let out a wail.

"Go look. Dey all right." She pointed toward the next room, then stooped to pick up her own little one.

Following behind Micah, Eliza almost bumped into him when he stopped abruptly. She peered around his shoulder into the dim interior of what was hardly more than a closet, where sleeping pallets were crammed so closely together that not a spare inch of floor remained. Grubby, ragged blankets were strewn every which way among the lot. A lump rose in her throat.

On one mattress, two slumbering girls, about six and three years of age, clung to one another in sleep, their thin bodies still racked by occasional sobs.

Micah turned to Eliza, his expression taut with concern. And without another word, he took another quilt from the three remaining and spread it over the motherless sisters.

❧

"I've never witnessed such despair," Eliza murmured a short time later on the homeward journey, her thoughts still on the impoverished recipients of the quilts. The rest of the coverlets had been distributed to other needy families.

"You might be surprised to hear that many of these folks are well-educated and had highly respectable jobs in their homelands," Micah answered evenly, his light brown eyes warm in the fading light. "But they left everything they had just to come to America. Home, family, friends, their livelihoods, all in hope of providing their children with a better life in a new country. Granted, a few are in such poor health the voyage itself claims them before they ever reach our shores. And with the lack of nourishing food, the rest are susceptible to any sickness that comes along."

"But the children! They haven't proper clothes. Some of them look as if they haven't seen a bathtub in months, if ever. And I even saw a rat scurrying along the hallway of that building. How can people continue to live in such squalor?"

"They've nowhere else to go. Most don't even speak the language when they first arrive. They're dependent upon go-betweens, often ministers or social agents, who set them up in language classes and find jobs for them—usually work no one else will do. The immigrants labor hard and long, and in time some of them actually do save enough money to start businesses of their own. But sad to say, those are often the minority."

"And those little girls whose parents passed away. What will become of them?"

"That's a common occurrence here in the tenements. That pair is lucky, since family friends will assume the responsibility of caring for them. So many in similar situations are left to fend for themselves. Child Placement shelters quite a number of orphans until we can find new families willing to adopt them. And, of course, there are other asylums in the city with similar facilities."

"But it's. . .it's just overwhelming."

"My sentiments exactly. And more shiploads arrive every day."

By the time the buggy pulled up outside Harper House,

Eliza felt completely spent, emotionally as well as physically. It was all she could do to make her way up the front walk.

Micah took hold of her elbow and assisted her. "Well, thanks again. I appreciate your willingness to help me today. I could have gone alone, but as I mentioned before—"

"I understand. Truly. The experience was rather enlightening, to say the least. I shall never complain again."

His lips spread into a smile.

Eliza glimpsed then, for a brief moment, Micah Richmond's soul, the depth of his caring and the concern that motivated him to work beyond the normal hours of his employment. And she fully understood his calling. She wanted to say something to commend him for his efforts, something profound, but nothing worthy enough came to her weary mind.

The door opened then, and Aunt Phoebe leaned out into the snowy air, some of the flakes landing on the crocheted shawl worn about her shoulders. Worry creased her face. "There you are, at last, Eliza! I was wondering what had detained you."

"The fault is all mine, dear lady," Micah explained. "I imposed on your niece's good nature to help me out this afternoon. Which she did most graciously, I must say."

"I'm just glad you delivered her safely home. Would you like a cup of hot tea before you go?"

"No, but thank you kindly. I'm expected at Anabelle's." He switched his gaze to Eliza as she was about to enter. "Again, I can't thank you enough for filling in for Mrs. Wilson. I'll endeavor not to take advantage of you again."

She merely smiled. "Good evening. Give Ana my love when you see her, and tell her that her presence was sorely missed at the sewing circle."

"I'll do that. Good evening to you both." Touching the brim of his bowler, he gave a polite tip of his sandy head and returned through the falling snow to his buggy.

Eliza stepped into Harper House, its golden lamplight casting intricate shadows among the finery, and closed the door. Hanging up her warm wrap, she turned, her gaze drinking in the array of splendor before her. And she closed her eyes in reproach. *All of this, for two people.*

There had to be more she and Aunt Phoebe could do to help.

seven

After a short visit with Anabelle and her parents, Micah returned to his rented room on Columbus Avenue. . .the sum total of his living quarters the past few years. Reluctant to spend the time or money it would require to keep up his late parents' sprawling house, he had leased it out to a young couple with a growing family and moved his personal things into a one-room apartment in a row of brick town homes. Simple and cheerless, it at least freed him from having to get caught up in repairs and other mundane chores involved with owning property.

Now, alone with the ticking of the mantel clock and the slowly dying embers of the fire he'd lit earlier, Micah rose from his knees and extinguished the bedside lamp before climbing between the cool sheets on his bed. The light snow which had begun earlier that afternoon now fell in earnest outside, muffling the normal night sounds in almost eerie stillness. And because he wasn't especially tired, it seemed a good time for reflection. Retrospection.

He couldn't help but think back on his day, on the heart-rending thankfulness expressed by the recipients of the latest quilts. Having just prayed for those folks and so many others with whom he'd dealt over the past several months, he imagined them warm and toasty beneath the thick coverlets provided by the nimble-fingered ladies of Faith Community Church.

He also thought of newly orphaned Rosa and Gabriella Riccio, who'd found refuge with family friends, the Garibaldis. But with the kind couple already stretched to the limit with an abundance of offspring of their own, Micah could only hope and pray that the sad little girls would adjust to life without their parents and not be too much of a drain on the Garibaldis.

And he could not entirely dismiss from his consciousness the memory of Eliza Criswell's presence this afternoon. He knew the young woman's gentle upbringing had sheltered her from the sort of reality found in Manhattan's lower East Side and most likely she'd been shocked over the whole grievous situation. But thinking back, something else had also been obvious. She hadn't appeared sickened or repulsed by what she'd seen. Instead she'd seemed touched. Humbled. Most especially, her heart had gone out to the little Riccio sisters.

Once during the ride homeward, he'd even caught the shimmer of tears in those wide blue eyes of hers, though she'd pretended a smattering of snowflakes had stung her face on a gust of wind. Micah sensed that the immigrants now had another concerned ally on their side, and a very beautiful one, at that.

With chagrin, he willed his thoughts to Anabelle, suffering through a cold, her pert nose pink and puffy, her eyes watery, sipping endless cups of tea laced with glycerine and honey to soothe her sore throat. Micah had grown up knowing her. She'd been a part of his life for as far back as he could remember. They shared a multitude of each other's secret dreams and fears and felt completely at ease with each other.

If only she understood his calling.

He had invited—all but begged—her to come with him upon occasion when he'd needed to drive to the tenements. But her constant refusals stopped just short of being adamant. Not only did Ana not wish to go there, she was just as determined about him finding some new line of work. Eventually he'd given up asking.

Every night he prayed with renewed fervor that she would have a change of heart, become burdened for the sad, never-ending stream of America's newcomers and share in his ministrations to them. How else would their marriage last? Until he was convinced that his life's work would not cause strife between them, he was in no hurry to take that step.

Realizing that his eyelids had grown heavy, Micah slowly filled his lungs and rolled over, nuzzling into the warmth of his own blankets as remembrances of this day's most pleasant companion crept into his thoughts. Again.

"My goodness, but you're quiet this morning." Aunt Phoebe's voice came from across the breakfast table.

Eliza became aware that she had yet to take a sip of coffee from the cup she'd been holding for who knew how long. "Sorry, Auntie. I suppose my thoughts were occupied elsewhere." Sampling the now-lukewarm liquid, she set it down and took up a square of toast, spreading on a thin coating of marmalade.

"Elsewhere. I see." The older woman's discerning blue gaze didn't miss much. "Considering you've been like this ever since you returned late yesterday afternoon, it must have something to do with that 'errand of mercy' Micah took you on."

Eliza tried to smile but failed miserably as her eyes filled with tears. "You have no idea how those poor people live, Aunt Phoebe. If you could just see the shabby hovels they are forced to call their homes, smell the filth, listen to the hopeless crying of children. It's far more than I can bear. Especially—" About to blurt out a bold remark about their own overabundance of blessings, she bit her lips and averted her gaze to her toast once again.

"Oh, but I have seen some of what you experienced, child," her aunt said softly. "Up until it became difficult for me to get around the way I could in my younger years, I was far more active in acts of benevolence. Personally, I might add."

The news surprised Eliza and also filled her with remorse. "I'm sorry. I had no idea. But don't you find yourself wishing you could do more? I mean, here we are, living in this grand old home, just the two of us, when not so very far away there are needy folks who exist with practically nothing. And more of them, it seems, arriving every week."

"Yes, it is a shocking reality. Which is why, even I, an old woman, endeavor to keep contributing all the funds this shop brings in. Little as it is, it's the best the Lord has enabled me to provide at this time in my life." Her aged face gentled with a wistful smile. "Truth is, I'd love to wrap up in a warm shawl and pull the rocker up close to the hearth for the simple joy of basking in ease. But as soon as I did that, we'd run out of stationery or hankies or scarves or some other item that brings in money I wouldn't have otherwise. Do you know what I'm saying?"

Eliza nodded. She had misjudged this kind relative and could only hope she hadn't hurt her as well. Coupled with the distress she'd felt ever since yesterday, it made it even harder to contain her unshed tears. "Please, forgive me for speaking out of turn. This is just so completely new to me that I'm having trouble dealing with all the emotions I'm feeling inside."

"I know, dear. How it must grieve the very heart of God to witness the often needless suffering of those unfortunates. I believe that must be why He lays the burden on the occasional younger, stalwart heart, like Micah Richmond. Through that sensitive man and others of similar character He is able to accomplish much more than we can ever realize to alleviate some of the woes of the poor."

Eliza chewed the last bite of toast in thought. Yes, Micah had a personal hand in what she now viewed as an incredible ministry. Never had she met such an unselfish, giving young man. Anabelle was truly fortunate to know she would one day wed such a champion of the downtrodden.

Champion. For all his advantaged upbringing, he had no qualms about picking up and hugging a dirty, ragged child. On the contrary, little ones ran to him with their arms outstretched, their eyes shining with adoration. It made quite a picture. . .one

Eliza did not expect would ever completely fade from her most priceless memories.

Then, conscious that harboring such notions about her best friend's fiancé was bordering on betrayal, Eliza purposely pushed all thought of Micah Richmond from her consciousness.

As she had a thousand times since yesterday.

❧

"Splendid!" Anabelle turned away slightly to dispose of her sniffles in her handkerchief before replacing it in the pocket of her indigo skirt. "You've been practicing."

"Yes, an hour a day actually." Eliza rested her fingertips lightly on the ivory keys. "I've been committing to memory those pieces you loaned me on Sunday."

"And it shows. Well, my friend, all I can say is that if you continue to keep at it, I'll not be of much use as your teacher. After all, this skill is acquired through diligence and single-mindedness."

"I know. Practice, practice, practice," Eliza said wryly. "Seems I've heard that before. But somehow, I don't seem to mind it now as I did when I was young and flighty. I've even enjoyed the scales, tiresome as I once thought them to be." She began at the beginning again, playing smoothly through the piece. The lilting melody resonated back from the papered walls of the sitting room.

Out of the corner of her eye, she saw Anabelle tuck her chin. "Were you very flighty? I find that hard to imagine. You've appeared so serious since you came here to live."

Thinking back on her arrival, not to mention the reasons for her hasty departure from Harrisburg, Eliza could only agree. "Well, I hope I haven't put you off with my dreary moods."

"Not at all. I haven't found you to be moody in the least. That word is better used to describe Micah these days."

Eliza's fingers fumbled on a chord, and she stopped and turned to Anabelle. "He hasn't struck me that way at all."

Recognition dawned on Anabelle's fragile features, and her

brows arched higher. "Oh, yes. He told me he implored you to accompany him on his errand of mercy yesterday afternoon." She shuddered, and her jade eyes took on a pained look. "How you could subject yourself to go among those ragamuffins is a mystery. I could never do that. Never."

Observing her friend's dark expression, Eliza could not bite back the urge to speak out in Micah's defense. "I, too, looked upon the occasion with dread, almost regretting that I'd allowed him to persuade me. But once we reached the tenements and I actually saw the horrors those poor families suffer every day of their lives, I could not help but be moved to tears. They so need someone who cares, which Micah does most admirably. You'd have been extremely proud of him, Anabelle, the way he reaches out to them and makes them feel important."

"Indeed. Well, the fact is, he's not the only kindhearted soul who looks after their needs. He's just the one who seems to draw his very life's breath from doing so." Ana gave a huff of consternation. "I do sorely wish he'd pass that *burden* on to someone else." Shuffling determinedly through some music sheets in her tote, she drew one out. "Here, try this. It's becoming quite the rage."

"Sweet Songbird of Love." Eliza perused the title as she tried to dismiss Anabelle's criticism of her fiancé. "Do you know the lyrics? I'll play it through once, and then you can sing as I go over it again."

Ana shook her head, her golden pompadour moving slightly with the motion. "Just play it, Eliza. I'm afraid I haven't much of a voice just yet."

"Oh. Of course. You're looking so well, I forgot you're still recovering from a cold."

Aunt Phoebe breezed into the room just then, bearing a silver tray with tea and cakes. "I thought you might enjoy some refreshments."

"Why, thank you, Auntie." Eliza rose and accepted the tray, placing it on a small, drop-leaf table by the window.

"Won't you have some with us?"

The older woman shifted her slight weight to her other foot. "Oh, I wouldn't want to intrude. It's pleasure enough to listen to the music drifting from here to the parlor. No sense in getting in the way of two young ladies who want to talk."

"We wouldn't mind at all," Anabelle assured her with a smile. "In fact, I'm sure we can prevail upon Eliza to play the new song I brought today."

❧

When at last the house had been locked for the night, the fires banked and curtains drawn, Eliza snuggled deeper into her fluffy bedding. The chilly air in her room hardly seemed noticeable as the blankets absorbed her warmth and multiplied it. *Part of the heat radiating from me surely must come from my face,* she thought in vexation. She had no right to be entertaining thoughts of Anabelle's beau. Nevertheless, visions of Micah Richmond had come unbidden to her mind amazingly often today.

He had reminded her so much of her own fiancé, Weston Elliot, when her aunt first introduced them. But Eliza couldn't picture Weston showing such concern for immigrants—or for anyone else other than himself, for that matter. His strong, patrician features at times seemed carved in stone, whereas Micah's possessed the ability to reflect an abundant range of emotions, depending on the moment. Weston would definitely frown upon that sort of spontaneity. Everything had to be kept to a strict schedule and work in precise order to suit him.

What had she ever seen in that egotist in the first place?

The question had come from nowhere, and Eliza gave herself a mental shake. Such ridiculous musings would be better spent if turned into prayers. So in the comfort of her warm bed, Eliza poured out her heart to God, trusting Him to make sense of the muddled ramblings of her overburdened mind as she lifted up two recently orphaned little girls in prayer.

eight

Despite a concentrated effort to occupy her every moment, Eliza found her thoughts returning time and again to the plight of Manhattan's underprivileged inhabitants—particularly to Rosa and Gabriella. Their heartbreaking loss caused a wrenching memory from Eliza's own past to surface. She'd been just a little child herself when her long-awaited baby sister fell prey to a fever and passed away in her infancy. A raft of girlish plans and dreams had been laid to rest with tiny Emily. But in her grief, Eliza had had loving mother arms to comfort her and dry her tears. She prayed that these two little ones would find solace with the kind friends who had taken them in.

Returning her attention to the violets she'd been embroidering on the front of a tea cozy, Eliza cast a critical eye at several uneven stitches and released a ragged sigh.

"Something troubling you, dear?" her aunt asked.

Already clipping the threads to make them easier to remove, she grimaced. "I'm afraid my mind insists upon wandering. I'll just have to redo this section."

The slight woman set her tatting on the lamp table beside her and got up. "Why don't we take a break? We've been laboring for more than an hour already, and I was just thinking fondly of some hot tea."

Eliza lay the scissors and tea cozy down and rose also. "I'd say that's a splendid idea. In fact, I'll even go and prepare it. I'll just be a moment."

"Thank you, dear. It does feel good to stretch these old legs a little after sitting for so long in one spot." She took a few cautious steps to the nearby window and moved a curtain panel slightly to peer outside.

Heading for the kitchen, it dawned on Eliza that her aunt's movements had lacked their normal perkiness. Perhaps an extra log on the fire would help dispel some of the dampness brought by the stormy sky. She'd see to that on her return.

The kettle on the back burner of the massive stove always retained a good supply of heat, so Eliza knew the water wouldn't take long to boil. She moved it to a hotter front burner, then went to the cupboard to take down the tea things. Soon enough, she returned to the workroom bearing the refreshment tray.

Just then, the doorbell trilled.

"I'll see to the customer, love," the older woman said. "You sit and enjoy your tea. Don't bother waiting for me."

Eliza nodded and watched after her aunt, noting the halting footsteps. The room did indeed seem chilly, so she crossed to the hearth and stoked up the fire, adding two small logs. On her way back, her gaze took in the dwindling supply of thread in the spool basket on the table between their chairs. With Aunt Phoebe occupied, it would take scarcely any time at all to run upstairs for more supplies before pouring the tea.

When Eliza opened the door of the spare room on the second floor, cold air wafted toward her from its unheated confines. She quickly found the needed thread and slipped several spools into her apron pocket. Turning, she glanced around as she strode slowly toward the door. Such a shame, a nice bedroom like this sitting virtually empty. It was larger than the one common sleeping chamber in the Garibaldi apartment. Yes, a true shame.

❧

"And so, dear friends," Pastor Norman said, focusing his attention on the congregation of worshipers, "it behooves us to remember what this passage in Matthew chapter twenty-five is telling us. 'I was an hungred, and ye gave me meat: I was thirsty, and ye gave me drink. . .'

"As I studied these verses in preparation for today's sermon,

I saw something quite interesting. Something I would like to point out to you, as well. Notice, the Bible says it was the *righteous* who didn't understand what Jesus was saying—the very people who are most apt to be conscious of doing service to God. The Lord had to explain the deeper meaning of His words to the people of His own flock. This is His answer: 'Verily I say unto you, Inasmuch as ye have done it unto one of the least of these my brethren, ye have done it unto me.' "

Peering up from the open Bible on his lap as the preacher droned on, Micah thought of scores of destitute folk he'd met since becoming associated with Child Placement. He had to admit that much was being done for them by a host of righteous people. Nevertheless, those efforts barely scratched the surface of what actually needed to be done. He couldn't help wondering, if every person who truly wanted to serve God did as much as humanly possible to relieve the circumstances of the immigrants, would there still be such deep need?

Even as he contemplated that question, Micah felt an even more disturbing one rise to the fore: Could he fault someone else, when he himself might not be doing as much as he possibly could? Perhaps his own efforts left much to be desired.

" 'Unto one of the least of these my brethren,' " the minister was saying, his voice cutting across Micah's musings, " 'ye have done it unto me. Come, ye blessed of my Father, inherit the kingdom prepared for you from the foundation of the world.' "

The man's discerning eyes surveyed his audience. "Next time you are faced with an opportunity to do good to someone less fortunate, beloved, think back on this passage of Scripture. Remember that the service you render unto others is, in reality, service to Almighty God. Can you do less than make it your very best?" He paused. "Let us bow in prayer."

The pastor's message rang a chord in Eliza's heart as Anabelle's fingers rendered a quiet postlude to the departing church members. All she could think about was that spacious, almost empty room at Harper House, whose purpose was for nothing more than cast-off furniture, cartons of unused items, and a selection of sewing supplies. Wouldn't it be of better service if occupied? Dare she even mention the notion to Aunt Phoebe?

One look at the older woman's pale countenance at the close of the service, and Eliza immediately dismissed all thought of the spare room as she moved nearer and placed an arm about the bony shoulders. "Are you not well this morning, Auntie?"

She fluttered a veiny hand. "Oh, it's probably just a chill. Once I get home and take a nice rest, I'm sure I'll feel more like myself. You'll see."

But Eliza had her doubts. Gently taking her aunt by the arm, she maneuvered the dear woman past the clusters of widowed friends who normally waylaid her to chat and led her aunt toward the entrance.

"Good day, Eliza," Micah said, coming alongside. "And to you, Mrs. Harper. Always nice to see some bright faces on such a gloomy day."

"Yes, hasn't it been dreary of late?" Aunt Phoebe remarked, her voice lacking its usual vibrancy.

Eliza watched concern register in the young man's expression as he centered his attention on her aunt, then flicked a questioning glance to her.

"I'm afraid Aunt Phoebe is feeling a bit under the weather. I'm taking her out to the buggy."

Without hesitation, he sprang to the opposite side and offered his arm. "Then I shall be honored to assist." He steered them around the departing worshipers bidding good-bye to the pastor and pushed the door open with his free hand.

"Fuss and bother," Aunt Phoebe muttered, but a sparkle in her eye belied her frown. "A simple chill is nothing to concern oneself about."

"Perhaps not," he said. "Nevertheless, we shall see that

you get home as quickly as possible."

When they reached the bottom step and the driver of the buggy pulled forward to the end of the walk, Micah effortlessly picked Aunt Phoebe up and deposited her onto the leather seat, then assisted Eliza and spread the lap robe over them both. "I'll check in on you later," he said, touching the older woman's sleeve, then nodded to Eliza and the driver.

A flick of the reins set the gelding in motion.

The sincerity she'd glimpsed in Micah's hazel eyes touched Eliza deeply, and she drew much comfort in knowing he truly cared about her aged aunt. No doubt his prayers would join her own wordless pleas for the older woman's welfare.

And perhaps God, in His mercy, would grant renewed health one more time. Trying to rest upon this assurance, Eliza swallowed and relaxed against the upholstery.

Once they reached Harper House, Eliza paid the stocky driver and hopped down from the buggy.

He followed a second later. "Always glad to lend a hand to fair ladies," he said in explanation, and gently helped Aunt Phoebe to alight and guided her to the door.

"Thank you, kind sir," the older woman whispered, utterly spent.

"Yes. Thank you so much." With a grateful smile, Eliza ushered her aunt inside and to her bedroom, thankful that the older woman occupied a first-floor chamber. She dispensed with both their outer wraps as Aunt Phoebe sank onto her feather bed.

"There, that's better," Eliza crooned. "Let me cover you up, then I'll go make some nice broth and tea for you."

"Later, perhaps," came her aunt's labored whisper. "I'll sleep now." And almost as soon as her silvery hair touched the pillow, her eyelids fluttered closed.

Not quite ready to take her leave, Eliza remained where she was for several moments, listening until the uneven breaths became more regular. Then she tiptoed out, leaving the door slightly ajar.

The big house seemed unnaturally quiet at this hour, even though Aunt Phoebe's Sunday naps had been a custom since before Eliza's arrival. She felt at a loss and paced the sitting room aimlessly as she tried to relinquish control of the situation to the Lord. *Please, please, Father. . .make her well again. She has so much to do here. . . .*

True to his word, Micah Richmond stopped by a few hours later.

At the sight of him, Eliza's heart skipped a beat, but she convinced herself she'd have been just as glad to see any friendly face after being alone with her disquiet all that time.

He hung his coat on a wrought-iron hook just inside the door, followed by his scarf and bowler. "How's our patient faring?" he asked and blew into his chapped hands.

She shrugged, hugging herself. "She seems to be sleeping peacefully whenever I peek in on her. See what you think."

He nodded. "I stopped by her doctor's house on the way here. He wasn't home, but I took the liberty of leaving word for him to call first thing in the morning."

"Thank you. I—" At his kindness, the floodgates behind Eliza's eyes threatened to collapse. She'd successfully banked her anxieties in her aunt's presence, and then later when she'd been by herself. But now those defenses started to crumble, and the thought absolutely mortified her. She just couldn't fall apart now, not in front of Micah, of all people.

He seemed to sense her distress and took a step closer.

A jolt of alarm shot through Eliza. She almost expected him to put his arms around her.

But he merely gave her shoulder an empathetic squeeze. "Everything will be all right, my friend. As I prayed for your aunt on my drive here, a feeling of great peace came over me. I believe the Lord will bring her through."

Eliza blinked away telltale mistiness and managed a smile.

He stared for a few seconds, then, appearing satisfied, he

strode quietly up the hallway to the older woman's room.

The scent of his hair balm lingered in his wake, as did the warmth and strength of his touch.

Eliza scolded herself. *It was only a friendly gesture, for pity's sake.*

But, oh, the comfort her soul had drawn from it.

Quickly reining in her wayward imaginings before they turned utterly ridiculous, she attributed her momentary weakness to a touch of homesickness for her demonstrative parents. She must have missed a hundred hugs since she'd left. . .some of which should have been Weston's embraces.

Weston. No doubt all of his displays of affection were lavished on Melanie now. . . .

Surprisingly, that thought didn't carry the usual sting. *That saying about time and its healing powers must be true.*

An almost imperceptible squeak from the other end of the hall brought Eliza back to the present. But before she could compose herself, her breath caught as Micah came into view. *Oh, Anabelle. I sorely wish you had come, too.* "H–how is she?"

"Resting quietly, as you said. Her color appears to be improving also."

Eliza touched a hand to her throat in relief. "Truly?"

Micah nodded. "She awakened for a few moments, so I offered a short prayer, and that seemed to comfort her. She drifted off to sleep again."

"Well, thank you. For coming, I mean. I know my aunt thinks the world of you."

"And I of her." His expression turned unreadable. "You share some of your aunt's finer qualities, you know."

The heat of a blush crested Eliza's cheeks. Speechless, she had no idea whether to accept the statement or challenge it. She said nothing.

If he noticed her reaction, Micah gave no indication as he crossed to the wall peg, took down his coat, and pulled it on.

"Well, the doctor should come by in the morning. I'll keep the two of you in my thoughts and prayers this eve."

"Thank you," Eliza murmured, knowing he should leave, wishing he would stay, and aware that she had no right to wishes concerning Micah Richmond.

And with a buoyant wave, he was gone.

nine

Eliza peeked in at Aunt Phoebe, then went upstairs to her own room. Her cheeks still burned with shame at the brazenly wanton thoughts regarding Micah. Falling to her knees beside the bed, she clasped her hands and bowed her head.

Dear heavenly Father, I'm truly mixed up and have no one to turn to except You. I beg Your forgiveness for my foolishness. When Weston tossed me aside, I almost hated him—as much for breaking my heart as for depriving me of Melanie, my dearest friend in the world. But with the passing of days and weeks, I realized I had no choice other than to accept my sad fate. With Your help, and Aunt Phoebe's kindness and love, I've done just that. I no longer harbor ill feelings toward Weston. I don't love him or hate him, and I'd rather spend the rest of my life alone than to be that vulnerable ever again.

But what I cannot understand is why I feel so drawn to Micah Richmond. I do not want someone to replace Weston—and it's not as if he were inclined to do so anyway. He's not free, Father. He belongs to Anabelle, and she is the best friend I have in this world just now. Please help me not to be untrustworthy or unfaithful to this new friendship.

I'm just being a silly goose, and I know it. So, please, help me to think clearly again and act rationally. Don't let me lose myself to daydreams and fantasies. I want You to fill all the needs of my heart. Help me to be the person You want me to be, and may my life glorify You always.

A new peace came over Eliza, enveloping her in its warmth. She stood to her feet and removed her Bible from the bedside table, then sank into the comfort of the chaise. Opening to the book of Psalms, she feasted upon the bounty before her.

❧

"My, but you seem preoccupied this evening," Anabelle remarked, setting the tray of scones and tea on the lamp table. She smoothed her butternut gabardine skirt with her fingers.

Micah gave her a one-sided smile and took her hand, drawing her down to the settee next to him. "Forgive me, sweetheart. I was just thinking of Mrs. Harper. She had a spell this morning at church."

"Oh, yes." Snuggling closer, she rested her golden head against his shoulder. "I thought I noticed Eliza leading her away after the service, rather than allowing her to visit with the other ladies as she normally does." She turned her face upward, meeting his gaze. "Is it something serious? Has there been word?"

He traced a finger lightly along her delicate jawline, catching the sincerity in her eyes, and his heart contracted. "I really couldn't say, just yet. I stopped by the house on my way over here to see how she's doing. She seemed to be resting and looked a little better than she did at church. I prayed with her and left. No doubt the doctor will run by there tomorrow."

"Then I shall pray for her tonight when I go to bed. How was Eliza coping?" she asked casually.

"Same as always. Had her aunt all tucked in bed with a tea tray waiting for when she awakened. Naturally she's worried, but she seems determined to leave the matter in God's hands."

Ana gave a consenting nod. A quiet moment elapsed before she spoke again. "Eliza is very. . .lonely."

"Think so?"

Another nod. "She left all her friends behind, you know, in Harrisburg. I think she's getting a bit homesick."

"Could be."

"I wish she'd agree to attend some Christmas concerts

with us. In the company of, say, Phillip Madison. Or even Charles Sprocket. A foursome would be such fun."

"Why don't you suggest it?" Even as he asked, Micah tried to picture gentle Eliza in the company of slick-handed Phillip or nasal-voiced Charles. He grimaced.

Ana toyed with the lace edging on her ivory silk sleeve. "Oh, but I have. She says she's not in the least interested."

"Well, then, we should accept her decision."

Leaning forward, Anabelle poured tea into the china cups, handing one to Micah. She added her customary two sugar lumps to hers and stirred it, the spoon making soft clicking sounds with her movements. Then she took a sip and set her cup down again. "I think Eliza was jilted."

Micah swallowed too quickly and held his breath as the scalding liquid singed his throat. He took a bite of a raisin scone, trying to envision the kind of rat who could inflict pain on someone like Eliza.

"She hasn't told me so," Ana admitted. "At least, not in so many words. But she's alluded to something sad. I'm sure she'll come out with the whole story one of these days."

"Let's wait, then. No sense making up stories that might or might not be true."

"And in the meanwhile, why don't you check with Phillip or Charles and see if either of them would consider escorting our new friend about town? I'm sure if I keep after her, Eliza will agree to join us."

"Whatever you say."

"Splendid." A sweet smile spread across Anabelle's lips.

❧

"Oh, I think complete bed rest for a week or so should suffice," Doctor Jenson said, tucking his instruments into the old black bag he'd brought with him before slipping into his equally worn black suit coat.

"A week!" Aunt Phoebe groaned.

"Only a week?" Eliza could not mask her elation that her

aunt's spell hadn't been more serious. Or that it hadn't been her imagination that the older woman looked more like herself this morning, even if a touch pale. Thinning hair draped the shoulders of her nightdress in two slender braids.

"That's what I said, ladies. A week." The white-haired old man winked at Eliza, then glared pointedly through his monocle at his patient. "And you'd best follow my orders, Phoebe, or I'll put you in the hospital myself. You manage to get yourself in a fix every year at this time, seems like, working yourself to death for that shop out front."

"Well, if I didn't, there'd be a lot of people without gifts for Christmas," she said in her own defense. After the good night's sleep, her voice had regained some of its force.

"Be that as it may, I expect you to stay in bed. This niece of yours appears perfectly capable of seeing to business." He glanced at his silver pocket watch, then tucked it into the fob pocket of his vest. "I'll check back day after tomorrow to see how you're doing. Good day, Phoebe. Miss."

"Thank you, Doctor." Eliza came around from the other side of her aunt's bed. "I'll show you out." As she led the way, she had to ask the question, had to satisfy herself. "She's really going to be all right? She's just overtired?"

"That's right. Wears herself out every holiday season, regular as clockwork. The old gal must think she's still a spring chicken."

Eliza smiled. "Well, I'll see that she obeys your orders. You can count on me."

He flicked a teasing grin over his shoulder. "Kinda thought that, just looking at you. Good day, miss." Plunking his hat atop his head, he nodded and took his leave.

Eliza all but skipped back to her aunt's room.

❧

The next morning Eliza had the shop dusted and open for business bright and early and discovered she enjoyed dealing with the customers, many of whom asked after her aunt and expressed their regards. Mostly women, they appreciated the quality of the goods. Eliza took singular pleasure when a patron would stop to admire something she'd done herself.

"Does this tea towel come in other designs?" a heavy-set lady asked as she browsed among the wares that afternoon, perusing, touching this and that with plump, bejeweled fingers.

"Yes. In fact, we've a selection of floral patterns in stock. Let me show you." Crossing to her, Eliza bent to open a drawer beneath the display of towels and brought out several others for the woman to examine.

After some consideration, she pursed her lips and inclined her head. "I'll take these two. My daughter's to be married in the spring. She loves getting pretty things for her hope chest."

"Then you've made a fine choice. A young wife would be proud to have these in her kitchen. Will there be anything else, madam?"

"Yes, that lily-of-the-valley tablecloth." Her index finger indicated the folded linen cover displayed to one side. "It's simply exquisite." She dug into her handbag.

Having finished embroidering the design in the cloth's four corners scarcely a week ago, Eliza tried not to blush as she wrapped the items and made change.

"Thank you, miss. Good day."

The bell above the door trilled on her departure.

Eliza swivelled to refold a few items that needed to be tidied before turning the *Closed* sign outward.

"So, how's our patient today?" Micah's resonant voice rang through the quiet room.

Eliza jumped, inadvertently knocking a stack of crocheted doilies to the floor. Before she could stoop to gather them, he beat her to it and handed them over with a smile. "Forgive me. I didn't mean to startle you."

"No harm done. I–I just didn't hear anyone come in," she said inanely, hating the flush rising upward from her collar.

"I happened to arrive just as that last lady was leaving."

"I see." Eliza's hands began an irritating tremble. Hoping it was not obvious, she reached to tuck a loose strand of hair into her hair net, then purposely laced her fingers together behind her back.

"Thought I'd stop by for the weekly donation," Micah went on. "But first I'd like to see Mrs. Harper, if I may."

"Of course." Gradually regaining her equilibrium, Eliza smiled. "The doctor's making her stay in bed all week, so she's a mite testy, but I'm sure she'll be happy to see you."

"Splendid." He spun on his heel and stepped into the hall.

His temporary absence gave Eliza a chance to call herself a few names for being so flustered. *A fine way to act,* she thought scathingly, *considering that fervent prayer just last eve.* She simply had to conquer her silly tendency to go all aflutter whenever Micah Richmond appeared. To start with, she drew several calming breaths, which did help. She repeated the procedure off and on while he remained with her aunt. *He is merely a friend,* she lectured inwardly. *A friend who is spoken for.* "And you are a goose," she added for good measure.

"Did you say something?" Exactly when Micah had exited Aunt Phoebe's room would remain a mystery, but those long strides of his quickly brought him into the parlor.

Eliza turned her eyes skyward. "Counting," she blurted. "I was merely counting stock." *Bother. Now I'm resorting to lying? This just has to stop.*

"Oh. Well, it appears the Lord has seen fit to answer our prayers and restore your dear aunt to health once again."

The small reminder of the Lord's constant presence reinforced Eliza's guilt. "Yes. I'm so thankful. She was able to take some broth and toast earlier. And I can tell from her temper she'll soon be back to feeling like herself."

He chuckled, a warm, low rumble that made Eliza smile.

"I'll get the funds she left for you." Aware of his gaze following her movements, but unable to do anything about it,

Eliza somehow managed to get to the drawer and find the packet quickly. She held it out to him.

A broad grin appeared as he closed his fingers around the envelope. "I do thank you immensely. Both of you. As I mentioned before, everything helps."

"I've been wondering, have there been any new developments for the little girls since our visit? Rosa and Gabriella, I mean?"

Micah tipped his head slightly in thought. "I was there just yesterday, actually. The family's doing their level best to cope with the extra mouths to feed, now that there's less income to live on. It's not easy, by any stretch of the imagination."

"Do you. . .do you think they'll be all right?"

"I sincerely hope and pray so, but only time will tell." He regarded her evenly. "You really do care about them, don't you?"

She had to be honest. "How could I not? Such heartbreak to deal with at such a young age."

"But that's only two out of thousands. We can only do what we can do and trust that it helps." He paused, pocketing the funds from Aunt Phoebe. "Guess I'll be off. Thanks again, Eliza. You'll be in my prayers."

And you will be in mine, her heart answered.

As the bell jangled above the door, a second, smaller one sounded from Aunt Phoebe's room. Eliza turned the *Closed* sign outward and went to answer the summons.

ten

By closing time the following afternoon, Eliza's feet ached from having been on them all day. It seemed the nearer it got to Christmas, the more customers came to buy gifts. No wonder Aunt Phoebe had been so worn out, she conceded, what with tending the shop most daylight hours and then working on projects until late at night.

Eliza bristled to think she had allowed the older woman to carry most of that burden, while she herself traipsed off to quilting circle every week, practiced the piano most mornings, and whiled away untold hours that could be better spent in making Aunt Phoebe's life easier. After all, hadn't that been the reason she'd come to New York in the first place?

Grimacing at her thoughtlessness, Eliza went to turn the *Closed* sign around. Her frown turned into a smile at the sight of a visitor coming up the walk, and she threw open the door to admit her friend. "Anabelle! How nice of you to come by!"

Ana handed her a basket of baked treats. "I thought you might be in need of some company."

"Oh, I am, I am. With the exception of Aunt Phoebe, I see only strangers most of the time. And thank you for the goodies. I'll make us some tea."

"While you do that, I'll look in on the dear lady, if you don't mind. I've brought her a book of poetry. I'll be just a few moments."

"How sweet of you. She will love it, I'm sure."

With a hopeful smile, Anabelle hooked her wrap over one of the wall pegs, tucking her gloves into the hood before removing a small wrapped book from the pocket. Straightening her jade gown, she went down the hall.

Eliza headed for the kitchen and got out the teapot, tidying up a few things she'd been too busy to care about while the shop was open. By the time the water was boiling and she had measured tea into the silver tea ball and filled the pot to the brim, her visitor joined her.

Anabelle pulled out a spindle-back chair and sat down. "As Micah reported, your aunt seems to be improving. I didn't stay long, though, lest I tire her. He's been quite anxious about the two of you."

"Your Micah tends to worry about a lot of folks," Eliza replied. "I just wish we hadn't added to his concerns." She set out matching cups and saucers, then brought the teapot to the table and placed it between them. "I could have jumped for joy when the doctor said Aunt Phoebe's just worn out—although I must confess, I feel somewhat responsible."

"Why is that?"

"I could have done so much more to help, but instead, I chose to occupy myself with my own activities. That had to be a factor in her having taken ill." Watching Ana's expression cloud over, she pressed on. "So, I've decided to stop going to the sewing circle—at least until after the holidays."

"Oh, I'm sorry to hear that. I do understand, though." She paused. "Just don't become a recluse yourself. That's one of the reasons I came by, actually."

Eliza frowned in curiosity.

"Micah and I would like you to attend a holiday concert with us. Us and a friend. A foursome, you know."

"A *gentleman* friend?"

Anabelle nodded, raising a hand to dismiss all of Eliza's objections. "It's just for an evening. I can't bear for you to be sequestered at home for the rest of the Christmas season when so many churches put on festive programs. And afterward we can go to some quiet spot for pie and coffee."

"I don't know. . . ."

"Come on, Eliza. I promised Micah I would be able to

persuade you to accompany us."

Envisioning herself in some quiet little spot across the table from Micah Richmond did strange things to Eliza's insides. But, her conscience reasoned, perhaps that was just what she needed. Being in his company when he was with Anabelle. Watching the two of them making doe eyes at one another. Witnessing their mutual love. It might just render a mortal blow to her absurd fantasies about the Weston Elliot look-alike.

Against her better judgment, she acquiesced. "All right. As soon as Aunt Phoebe can be left alone for an evening, I'll go out with you—*and* your gentleman friend."

A new glow filled Anabelle's eyes. "Splendid!"

"But only once," Eliza amended.

"As you wish. I can't wait to tell Micah!"

But even as Eliza poured the tea, she hoped fervently that she wasn't making a huge mistake.

❧

Eliza brushed out her aunt's silvery hair, fashioning it into its customary knob at the crown. She fluffed a few loose tendrils around her face, then stepped back to assess her work. "I do declare, you're looking positively chipper this morning, Auntie."

Crossing her arms over her bosom, the older woman emitted a huff. "All I know is it feels downright ridiculous to have to spend one more day in this bed with Christmas a scant three weeks away. I need to be up and doing more than just crocheting."

"Now, now," Eliza scolded good-naturedly. "You know what Dr. Jenson said. You don't want him to hustle you off to the hospital, to be poked, prodded, and peered at, when a few more days' rest will only help you to get stronger."

"Yes, yes, I've heard that lecture more times than I care to admit. I'll stay here, more's the pity, but I don't have to like it." She made a face at the books on the bedside table. "Are there any more classics in Cap's library? I've read these a dozen times already."

"I'll take a look. I'm sure there must be something. Have you finished the poetry book Anabelle brought?"

"Twice." Her countenance softened with a smile. "It was sweet of her to come by and wish me well, though, her and Micah. They'll make a good match—assuming he ever gets down to marrying the girl, that is. Can't imagine why he's dragging his feet."

Eliza didn't respond, instead stepping to the window and opening the draperies to allow the bright sunshine in. "Looks like another glorious day. No doubt dozens of customers will come by the shop."

"How's the stock holding up?"

"Fine, Auntie. Just fine. Stop worrying." Bending to bestow a kiss to her companion's silken cheek, she hugged her as well. "I'll bring your breakfast tray directly."

Her gnarled fingers squeezed Eliza's hand. "Do forgive my orneriness, dear. I truly appreciate your kind attention to an old lady. It's just—"

"I know," Eliza murmured gently. "It won't be much longer. The doctor's sure to notice how much you've improved since he was last here."

"Largely thanks to you," she admitted with a grudging smile. "Now, about my breakfast. . ."

Micah looped the horse's reins through the hitching post in front of the tenement building and helped his assistant to alight from the buggy. He handed her one of the sacks of groceries they'd brought and took the remaining two himself, and they started toward the cluttered stoop directly ahead.

"Mercy," Mrs. Wallace exclaimed, her short legs stepping over a greasy-looking puddle in her path. "One naturally expects winter to improve a dreary spot, what with new snow falling from time to time."

"It'll take more than a few inches of snow to alleviate some of this gloom," Micah said dryly. "A raging blizzard, maybe."

The pleasant-faced woman chuckled, and the cheeks beneath her feather-trimmed hat plumped with her smile. Then she sobered. "Ah, but then some of these poor souls would have it all the harder, wouldn't they?"

Micah could only agree.

"Here," she offered. "I'll get the door. You have your arms full."

He grinned his thanks, and the two of them paused just inside while their vision adjusted to the dimness of the long hallway.

As always, children swarmed around them both, eyes wide and expectant. They did not, however, display a lack of manners by so much as hinting about the penny candy that typically appeared whenever Micah arrived with sacks. He rarely kept them waiting. Setting down one of his bags, he reached into his coat pocket and withdrew some peppermint sticks. "Here, Tony, Vinnie, Gina. One for everybody."

Beside him, Mrs. Wallace had her own cluster of youngsters vying for attention. "Little Rosa, Maria, Gabriella." She handed a treat to each one in turn, and almost en masse, the gaggle of little ones skipped away with their treasures. She turned to Micah. "Now, where do we start?"

He gave her a lopsided grin. "First two apartments, then the Garibaldi household." Gesturing with his head for her to follow, he strode toward the nearest flat.

Once a portion of the groceries had been delivered to the intended parties, he and Mrs. Wallace approached Gina and Vinnie's place. Micah rapped on the doorjamb.

The olive-skinned housewife appeared almost instantly. Looking more tired than usual, dark circles shadowed her eyes as she dried her hands on the soiled apron covering her faded dress and stepped aside. "Mr. Richmond. Mrs. Wallace. Come in'a, come in." She pretended not to notice the burden Micah held.

"Thought we'd come by and see how you're doing," he said evenly. "We hoped you might put some of this to good use." With that, he pressed the bulging sack into her arms.

Her dark eyes misted over, and she swallowed. "Oh, you shouldn't have done'a dis. But Vittorio an' me, we say *graci.*"

"How is everyone?" Mrs. Wallace asked.

The woman released a weary sigh. "Some days'a good, some days'a not so good. We make do."

"And the girls, Rosa and Gabriella," Micah prompted. "Are you managing all right with them?"

She cast a surreptitious look over her shoulder, as if not wanting to be overheard, then met his gaze. "I tell'a you, it'sa hard. We love dem, you know. But we got our own to feed and clothe. It'sa not easy to do for our own." A self-conscious shrug finished the unspoken thought eloquently.

Micah gave a reluctant nod.

"We try. We make do."

"I understand. That's all we could hope, right? I'll check back again in a few more days."

"You do dat. And *graci* for da food. . .and da caring. *Arrivederci.*"

"God bless," Micah said. He glanced at Mrs. Wallace, and they turned for the door.

Their footsteps echoed hollowly from one end of the deserted corridor to the other, all the way to the exit. Neither of them spoke until they reached the buggy.

"Well, I guess we know what that means," his companion said under her breath on a sigh of resignation.

Micah nodded. "Might as well start looking for a family who'd like to adopt two little Italian girls." But how, with so many prejudiced against their foreign culture, their Catholic faith? The best he could do for now was try to find a temporary shelter. And pray that God would touch someone's heart.

Handing Mrs. Wallace up to the seat, Micah gathered the traces and climbed in beside her. The afternoon was starting to cloud over again, and there was a definite nip to the air. He'd best drive her directly to the office before seeing to the errands that still awaited him.

For some reason—*most likely because she asked about the children only yesterday,* he told himself—his thoughts drifted to Eliza. This new development would likely disturb her almost as much as it did him. *If* he mentioned it, that is. She already had worries enough caring for Mrs. Harper. It might be prudent not to say anything.

If only Ana showed some of that concern, he mused in his despondency. Or even just listened sympathetically while he unburdened himself after a particularly trying day. After all, wasn't that part and parcel of being a wife?

When they married, she'd have to be more accepting of his ministry. If he could only convince her to go with him on one of his benevolent calls, she'd see he was involved in something of real value. Anyone with a heart as tender as Anabelle's could hardly escape being affected if she witnessed the deep need herself.

Releasing a shuddering breath, he turned the matter over to God in silent prayer.

eleven

When Aunt Phoebe at last dropped off to sleep, Eliza extinguished the downstairs lights and trudged upstairs to her bedroom. Every bone in her body ached, and her stomach growled from hunger, but she was too weary to care. A letter had come from home in response to her most recent missive, and she had yet to read it. Taking the envelope from the pocket of her skirt, she placed it on her bedside table and lit the lamp. Then she broke the seal and unfolded the pages, anticipating the memory of her mother's melodious voice in the neatly penned words:

Dearest Eliza,

Your father and I were so very glad to hear from you again. We miss you desperately but do understand your decision to remain in New York indefinitely. Our dear Phoebe has been alone far too long, and now that she is up in years, I know she must appreciate your company. I pray your presence will be a comfort and a blessing to her.

I hesitate to tell you this, daughter, but thought you should hear it from me rather than some other source. Melanie has come home, alone.

Eliza, caught completely off guard by the startling news, felt a chill run up her spine. Melanie, alone? What could have happened? Sympathy for her former best friend vied with the bitterness caused by the betrayal of their relationship. But even as her emotions warred within her, Eliza read on:

She refuses to talk to anyone and will not so much as set foot outside her room. She scarcely touches the lovely meals the housekeeper prepares for her, and her mother is beside herself with worry.

Melanie has taken no one into her confidence, so it is anyone's guess as to what occurred after she left town. I thought you should know about this, in the event you might chance to come for a visit.

Please take care of yourself, my darling, and give Phoebe our warm regards. Our prayers are ever with you.

With deepest love,
Mother

Barely able to draw breath, Eliza sank to her bed and let the crisp stationery flutter to the floor. She and the high-spirited Melanie had been bosom friends as far back as her memories of childhood reached. Together they had shared giggles and girlish secrets, tears, school years, and daydreams. And quite possibly the rift between them pained Melanie every bit as much as it did Eliza.

But, she reasoned, that did not alter the fact that Melanie had run off with Weston. If she had taken a butcher knife and cut out Eliza's heart, it could not have inflicted more pain.

Eliza filled her lungs and slowly let them deflate, knowing she should at the very least pray for the girl. And perhaps, in time, she would be able to do just that. But right now, Melanie Brown Elliot was one of two people in the world she could not bear to think about. All she wanted to do was rid her mind of all conscious thoughts and climb into bed.

"Here you are, Auntie. Your favorites." Eliza placed the bed tray before the older woman, then went to open the drapes.

"Thank you, dear. The coddled eggs look perfect. And you even remembered marmalade for my toast. Bless you."

With a thin smile in response to her aunt's cheerfulness, Eliza busied herself tidying the room. "Just ring the bell when you've finished, and I'll bring you your crocheting. Doctor Jensen said there's no reason why you shouldn't be permitted to do something that isn't strenuous." She turned to leave.

"Just a minute, child."

Pausing at the door, she swivelled to face her aunt.

"You look rather pale this morning. Did you not sleep well?"

"I'm fine," Eliza hedged, toying with a fold of her dark gray skirt. "I just have some things on my mind."

"Difficulties concerning the shop?"

She shook her head. "No, it's nothing for you to worry about."

"Well, should you need someone to talk to, you know where to find me." The old spark shone in Aunt Phoebe's eyes.

"Thank you. I'll remember that. Oh, I think I hear the bell. I'll be back to check on you in a little while."

Exiting the comfortable bedchamber, Eliza hastened to greet the day's first customer.

❧

Phoebe nibbled a corner off a triangle of toast, then set the tray aside. During these days of lying in bed with nothing to do but sewing, the thought had come to her to put together a surprise for Eliza, one fashioned after the Epiphany tradition Cap had brought to their marriage from his Anglican background. For twelve nights following Christmas, Eliza would be given a different present. By the time she opened the last gift, she would possess a carved wooden box with twelve heirlooms, special items Phoebe had cherished throughout her own life.

So far she had only come up with six gifts. But on the spur of a moment, she'd remembered her grandmother's ornate pill box necklace. It would make a perfect addition to the other things collected thus far: a tiny silver hand mirror her father had given to her mother on their wedding day; four matching pewter napkin rings from her mother's hope chest; a gilt-edged picture frame, a set of crystal knife rests, a hand-painted silk fan Cap had purchased on his first voyage to the Orient, and an ornate-handled letter opener.

With a sly smile, Phoebe swung her legs over the side of the bed and maneuvered her feet into the warm knitted slippers next to it before padding to her dresser. Hopefully the pill box would be somewhere in the middle drawer. All she had to do was find it and sneak it into the wooden box hidden beneath her bed before Eliza returned and caught her up. That would leave a mere five articles to be added.

She could hardly wait for Christmas!

As Eliza straightened up the dwindling displays on the various shelves in the gift shop, the door opened. Her heart lurched as Micah stepped inside on a blast of chilly air.

"Good afternoon, Eliza. Thought I'd check in on that aunt of yours again."

"How nice. She always enjoys seeing a friendly face." Eliza purposely kept her tone breezy, hoping to recapture her poise and waylay the maddening blush that seemed to appear so easily in Micah's company despite her best intentions.

"Hope I won't be disturbing a nap or anything."

Eliza shook her head. "I'm quite sure she's awake. I took in a lunch tray a little while ago, and she didn't appear tired in the least."

"Good." He loosened his coat, flashing a jovial grin on his way past, and his confident footsteps took him down the hall.

She plucked the feather duster from its hook and flicked it over a porcelain doll and a pair of crystal candleholders, her movements carrying her before an oval wall mirror that was accented by a spray of dried flowers positioned above. Catching her reflection, Eliza realized the smile she had given Micah Richmond had yet to fade. With an exasperated huff, she schooled herself into line and attacked her chore with more discipline.

It wasn't long before she heard Micah returning.

He bent to pick up a crocheted coaster that must have fallen during her dusting and handed it to her. "Thank the Lord your aunt appears to be a little more perky each time I come by. Amazing resilience, that lady."

Eliza had to agree. "Of course, she knew she had to follow the doctor's instructions to the letter or face me, cracking the cat-o'-nine-tails over her back," she said facetiously, replacing the coaster on the stack of others.

A teasing light gleamed in his eyes, and for a fraction of a second, Eliza thought she saw them wander over her. "How true. The moment we met I saw right through you, to that mean streak that runs a mile wide."

Her soft laugh couldn't have been held in check no matter how much she might have wished it, and a similar, deeper one rumbled from his chest. Yet for some reason she sensed everything was not as it appeared. She hesitated about questioning him but gave in to her intuition. "Is there something wrong, Micah?"

His expression took a somber turn, and he shrugged. "I wasn't going to mention it, particularly to you. Perhaps I shouldn't even have come."

A jolt of alarm seized Eliza. "Whatever do you mean? Is my aunt not doing well after all?"

He held up a calming hand. "Please believe me; she truly does appear to be recovering quickly. No, I'm afraid my concerns lie in other directions just now."

Continuing to study his demeanor, Eliza drew her own conclusions as the memory of two heartbroken little girls huddled together on a miserable pallet surfaced in her mind. "Well, if you're hesitant to say anything to me about it, I must surmise it has something to do with the children. Am I right? Has something happened to them?"

Micah inhaled a long breath, then slowly expelled it. He rested an elbow on the shelf beside him, meeting her gaze. "It. . .uh. . .has more to do with the Garibaldis, actually."

"They've decided they cannot continue to look after Rosa and Gabriella."

An amazed smile spread across his lips. "That's one thing I admire about you, Eliza. You're very astute. I came here for the express purpose of assuring myself that Mrs. Harper is improving—definitely not intending to involve you in my problems."

"Quite gallant of you, I must say. However, if that *problem,* as you call it, concerns those poor little girls, then I'm already involved. I've felt deeply burdened for them since the day I first saw them. You might very well come out with it. I must know."

Micah pressed his lips into a grim line and stepped to the window, his back to her as he looked outside. His shoulders sagged. "The Garibaldis have made every effort to incorporate the Riccio girls into their household. Done their level best. But lacking the income the girls' parents brought in, it's nigh impossible for them to make ends meet. Mrs. Garibaldi as much as asked me to start making other arrangements for those little ones."

A heaviness settled over Eliza's chest. "But it's almost Christmas," she murmured. "Surely they can stay where they are until after Christmas."

"And then what?" Micah asked, turning to face her. "I've already contacted everyone I can think of, and all for naught. It's precisely the approaching holidays that make it next to impossible to find a haven for Rosa and Gabriella right now. To be perfectly honest, I haven't the slightest idea what I can do to help them."

"Well, we'll just have to think of something, then, won't we?"

"We?" A half-smile lit Micah's compelling features.

Not to be undaunted, Eliza only repeated herself with more conviction. "We."

"When you think of something," he said flatly, "be sure to

let me know. I'm out of options at the moment. Even if I can't find a family who'll adopt them permanently, I need a place where they'll be looked after, a temporary shelter until a spot opens up for them. Our facility is filled to the hilt with other children in the same boat they are."

Eliza had surmised as much, but hearing the sad information again made the need seem even more acute. "I assume you've already made the matter public knowledge at church."

"Our church, Mrs. Wallace's church, and a raft of others."

"Well, then, we'll have to look elsewhere."

He chuckled, but without a hint of mirth. "No doubt you've a long list of places that fit the bill."

"Not yet. But I will." The strength of her certitude surprised even Eliza, yet she knew somehow that she would find a home for those girls, even if she had to build it herself!

Micah watched with fascination as it seemed as if the wheels inside Eliza's head turned like perfectly meshed gears inside a pocket watch. He really hadn't intended to dump this weighty matter on her slender shoulders. That had been the absolute last thing on his mind. He couldn't remember exactly how she'd managed to wangle the information out of him, but now that she had, it didn't seem quite so impossible. Nothing was changed. She knew even less people in the city than he did. But somehow he sensed the Lord would use her in this situation. He just didn't see how.

"Will you be calling on Anabelle this evening?" she asked out of the blue.

"Most likely. I go over there nearly every night. Her parents' sort of—"

"Splendid," she interrupted. "Then, would you please ask Ana if she can come over here tomorrow? Tell her I need her help."

"Whatever you say." Micah continued to stare, trying to decipher what was going on in that dark little head of hers, but at the moment he didn't have a clue. He cleared his throat. "Well, I'd best be going. I have some more calls to make this afternoon."

Tapping an index finger against her lips, she gave no indication she'd even heard him speak, but she nodded absently as she began pacing the floor.

"Uh, well, good day," he said, crossing to the door.

"Hm? Oh, yes. I'll be praying too. Something's bound to turn up. You'll see."

Slinging a glance over his shoulder, Micah chuckled under his breath and left. That young woman had come a long way from the timid, cowed soul he'd first met, and the change in her was utterly fascinating!

Whistling as he climbed aboard his buggy, he drove off.

twelve

"It's now or never," Eliza muttered to herself. She'd paced the floor between the gift shop and her aunt's room so many times, trying to work up courage to broach the subject uppermost in her mind, she was surprised there was no obvious path worn in the carpet runner. But now that the shop was closed for the day and her constant prayers only served to strengthen her resolve, it seemed senseless to put the matter off any longer. She sloughed off her nerves and quietly entered the bedchamber.

An imperceptible snore drifted across the dimly lit room.

Eliza rolled her eyes and tiptoed out again, closing the door after her. Of course Aunt Phoebe would doze off at times, lying abed all day. But all that gathering of courage, for nothing. Oh, well, it was her own fault for taking so long to make up her own mind.

The hearty smell of the pork roast Eliza had started earlier permeated the house, making her stomach growl. Had she even had dinner? The day seemed little more than a blur. Going to the kitchen, she peeled potatoes and carrots and set them to boil. Then she took a lamp and headed for the stairs.

She'd been inside the spare room a dozen times over the last few days, getting replacement supplies or putting some unused object out of the way. She noticed that the pattern in the wallpaper had faded over the years, but the wainscoting was still in good shape. The room had been ever so pretty back when her family had stayed here on visits. But standing in the doorway now, the lamp held high, she envisioned it as something far more noble than a mere guest room. It could easily be transformed into a haven for a needy child, or even two. Two little girls. A hopeful smile tugged at her lips.

But how would she convince Aunt Phoebe?

Taking a step further inside the shadowed depths, Eliza imagined it housing a double bed with colorful counterpane, a good-sized wardrobe, a rocking chair, and some bright curtains. Surely she could persuade Anabelle to help fix it up. And the two of them could sew some little dresses. . . . Each new plan gave birth to another, until Eliza feared her head would burst.

When Aunt Phoebe awakened a short while later, she appeared completely rested and more like her old self than she'd been for days. Eliza couldn't suppress the desire to compliment her. "You're looking wonderful, Auntie. How about coming to the parlor for supper? I'm sure Doc Jenson would approve if I helped you to the table and back afterward."

Some of the care lines vanished from the older woman's face. "Why, that's a splendid idea. I haven't had anything but these four walls to look at since Sunday. I'd dearly love a change of scenery."

"Then let me get your wrap and slippers." She snatched the flannel wrapper from where it lay draped over a chair back and helped her aunt into it, then supported her as she stepped one foot and then the other into the warm slippers.

They walked slowly up the hall, and reaching the parlor, Eliza seated her in a chair near the fire, then went to fill their plates with food. In no time at all they were enjoying the succulent pork with mashed potatoes and gravy and honeyed carrots.

"This is perfectly delightful," Aunt Phoebe said, touching her napkin to the corners of her mouth when she finished. "I couldn't eat another bite."

"Not even a sliver of pie?" Eliza asked. "One of your regular customers, a Mrs. Knight, brought over a fresh apple crumb pie and asked me to pass along her good wishes for your recovery."

At this, the elderly countenance gentled. "Why, how very

sweet of Mabel. I just might be able to down a small piece. With a cup of tea, if you don't mind. Maybe then you'll tell me what's on your mind."

In the process of rising to her feet, Eliza sank back down to her chair in surprise. "How did you know I wanted to talk to you about something?"

Her aunt smiled slyly. "When a person spends a good deal of her life dealing with the public, she becomes rather skilled at being able to read other folks."

Eliza shook her head in wonder. "I see. Well, I'll go get our dessert. Then we can talk."

Actually, she reasoned, it could be a good thing, her aunt's being so discerning. It saved her from having to think of a way to bring up the subject of the room.

As she poured the tea a short while later, Eliza retook her seat and sampled a bite of pie. She closed her eyes in delight.

"Mabel has a real way with pie, doesn't she?"

"It's excellent. I don't know when I've had better."

"So, what is it, child?" Aunt Phoebe took a cautious sip of the hot liquid and relaxed against the back of her chair in expectation. "Bad news from home?"

Eliza blanched. "I did receive some startling news from Mother, but this has nothing to do with that. It's a different matter entirely."

"Well, best you come out with it. That's the simplest."

Drawing a long, slow breath for fortification, Eliza plunged forth. "I hardly know where to start. You know about Micah's work and the frustrations he faces on a daily basis, trying to place orphaned children in a city that's already overcrowded."

"Yes, we've discussed the matter quite often."

"Well, until I actually made that visit to the tenements myself," Eliza said, "I hadn't the foggiest notion of the breadth of the problem. Now that I've been there and witnessed the sordid conditions, I feel almost guilty that we have so much, when others lack even the bare necessities."

"Which is precisely why I run the gift shop," her aunt reminded her. "So that I can help out in a tangible way."

"I know, Aunt Phoebe. Truly, I do. But don't you ever feel that it isn't enough? Don't you wish you could do more?"

"At my age? What more could I do, if I might ask?"

Eliza's pulse rate quickened, and her mouth went dry. She quickly gulped some tea and set down her cup. "I'm not asking you to do more, exactly. This is a project I would like to undertake on my own—with Anabelle's help, if she's willing."

Aunt Phoebe continued to stare but did not interrupt.

"It's the spare room," Eliza blurted. "I'd like to convert it into a child's room."

The older woman tucked her chin.

"Nothing permanent, mind you," Eliza quickly added. "But for those times when Micah's at his wit's end and needs a temporary shelter for one or two little children while he tries to find them a real home."

"But you don't know what you're suggesting! A child—children, here? At Harper House?" Her gaze making a swift circuit of the parlor shop, Aunt Phoebe seemed to center on all the breakable items, the shelves of fragile things that could meet their doom within a few seconds of a rambunctious child's entrance.

"I know what you're thinking," Eliza said placatingly. "But I really don't think a little girl would be much trouble. Or even two, at times. It would be just for a few hours, in some cases. Days, in others. With an assortment of playthings available for them to keep themselves occupied, they'd have no reason to venture down here and touch your things."

"Quite an interesting theory, I'd say," her aunt said without emotion. "Have you ever been responsible for little ones?"

"Not for an extended period of time, no. But I've been around enough of them to know that they will accept established boundaries when treated with respect and love and a firm hand."

Aunt Phoebe shut her eyes and rubbed the bridge of her nose under her eyeglasses in thought.

"And I don't foresee any problem with my plan. I think it's possible and worth a try, at the very least. Would you let me try, Auntie? For the sake of the children?"

She raised her eyelids and met Eliza's gaze. "Did he put you up to this? Micah?"

"No," Eliza said, shocked. "I never mentioned the subject to him at all, though I confess I've been considering my undertaking for several days now."

"I see." Her slight bosom rose and fell as her demeanor revealed troubled thoughts. "I must tell you, child, this whole notion of yours has caught me somewhat off balance."

Eliza didn't know how to respond. She remained silent.

"But I will pray about it—"

Blinding hope made Eliza smile. But the smile wilted as quickly as it had appeared once her aunt went on.

"That's the best I can promise. I know the need exists and is very serious. I also know I'm not physically able to deal with the noise and confusion or inconvenience of having little ones underfoot, but you are. For that matter, perhaps that's why the Lord brought you here in the first place. Not as an answer to my prayers, but to Micah Richmond's."

Eliza hadn't considered that possibility, but she had to give the suggestion merit. The ministry the young man was involved in was a very compassionate one, one that drew her in immediately and compelled her to do whatever she could to help.

"I'm quite tired now. Would you please help me back to my bed?"

"Of course, Auntie. And I won't bring up the subject again until after you've had a chance to pray about it."

An almost imperceptible nod seemed all she could manage.

❧

"So," Anabelle said brightly as she hung her cloak. "Micah

says you wanted to see me."

Eliza nodded. "Come into the kitchen, and we'll have tea while I bring you up to date on a matter I'm considering." Linking her arm through her friend's she drew the girl along.

After a little more than a quarter hour had passed, Eliza realized she had been talking on and on with scarcely an interruption, and that a peculiar expression had drawn Anabelle's fine brows together in a frown. Her cheeks appeared nearly as white as the shawl collar on her gown. "You don't care for my scheme?"

"That's putting it rather mildly, but you did ask." Ana wagged her head in disbelief, her pompadour shifting ever so slightly with the motion.

"But, don't you see?" Eliza pressed on. "It's a way to help those who can't help themselves. As Pastor Norman said in his sermon, it's a way to serve God. A very noble way. Children are very dear to His heart."

"Yes, but one must look at the more practical side. Think of your sickly aunt in this houseful of lovely things having to endure the excessive racket children seem so fond of."

"But—"

"And that's another thing," she went on, tapping the bowl of her spoon on the table for emphasis. "They wouldn't even be children of. . .well, of class. They'd be riffraff, Eliza. Ragamuffins. Dirty, likely infested with lice or other such disgusting vermin. Perhaps even ill."

"But no less dear to the Lord," Eliza countered. "One's class is of little import here in America. We're all equal. And as far as dirt, that would wash away in a bath, and then we could provide the ragamuffins with some decent clothing."

Anabelle regarded her steadily, then raised her chin a notch. "Micah couldn't interest me in his plight, so he's latched on to you. He put you up to this, didn't he?"

Stunned by her friend's accusation, Eliza vehemently shook her head. "No. Aunt Phoebe asked me the same question last eve, and I assured her as I'm assuring you, this entire thing is my idea. Micah knows nothing of it. I haven't mentioned it to him at all. There'd be no reason to unless my aunt agrees to it."

Appearing somewhat mollified, Anabelle's features softened to their more natural beauty. "Forgive me, Eliza. I get quite upset when Micah suggests I involve myself in his calling. But I simply cannot do it. I loathe filth of any sort, bad smells, and places where diseases are rampant. Nothing would make me happier than for him to find some other line of employment."

"I'm sorry to say, I see little chance of that," Eliza admitted in all honesty. "He truly cares for those poor little ones, Ana. And the Lord reaches out to them through Micah. I do wish you'd go with him once, just to see how he talks to them, how he loves them. You'd feel differently, I'm sure."

"I doubt that." A shudder racked Anabelle's slim shoulders. "I'll never set foot in those hovels. I will pray for those people. I'll sew quilts for them and contribute funds. I'll even endure having my betrothed going among them when it's necessary. But that's as far as my constitution will allow."

Watching her friend's expressive face, Eliza knew she'd spoken truthfully. Not everyone possessed the fortitude required to work among the lowly masses. Anabelle had a good heart, but it was one that needed to be in an environment that was clean and sterile. Letting out a breath she hadn't known she'd been holding, she patted Ana's hand. "Well, would you still help me to fix up an appealing room, if Auntie decides in my favor?"

"I can't see why I shouldn't. It could be a lot of fun, really."

"And perhaps you might be prevailed upon to sew some dresses and nightclothes from time to time?"

Grudgingly, Anabelle acquiesced. "If necessary."

"That's all I ask," Eliza said. But inside, she pitied her friend. She was so wrapped up in fear of the unknown, she could never know the joy that came from helping others.

thirteen

Phoebe watched Eliza fussing about the room without ever making eye contact in her hurry to straighten things up. The girl was trying so hard to pretend that this morning was no different from any other. But the request she'd made the night before hung between them like yesterday's wash.

From the day of her arrival, Eliza had been like a ray of sunshine in the gloom of her solitary existence, and she had so quickly grown used to her niece's presence she could hardly remember what life had been like before. Eliza was a huge help around the place, quickly mastering the skills needed to keep the shop stocked with popular items. And she took it upon herself to do chores before they were mentioned. Yet the girl had not asked anything for herself. Not until now.

Studying her, she saw that Eliza looked particularly fetching this morning, having donned a chocolate-colored morning gown with a printed design in shades of rust and gray. Switching her gaze from her niece's lissome form to the nearly finished breakfast before her, she raised her cup and took a hearty sip of the freshly brewed tea.

"Can I do anything else for you, Aunt, before I open the shop?" Eliza asked, finally looking her way.

"No, dear, I'm quite fine, thank you. But I would like to say something first."

Eliza's expressive features fell a few notches in uncertainty. She approached the bed and stood there, nervously twisting the handle of the feather duster in her hands, eyes bright with hope, her heightened coloring revealing the fragility of her dream.

"I've been giving a good deal of thought to your proposal, Eliza, along with conferring with the Lord about the matter."

Eliza moistened her lips.

"And I can't believe I'm actually saying this, but. . .I'm willing to give you the opportunity to do what you feel you must."

Her niece let out a tiny gasp. "Truly? Oh, Auntie!" Bending over, Eliza threw her arms about her and kissed her cheek. "Oh, thank you. Thank you. Anabelle and I will start looking for things we'll need right away."

"Before you go too much out of your way, check the attic. I did sell some of the furniture I wasn't using after Cap died, but I'm quite sure there's a sturdy bedstead, at least, and perhaps a few other items you might find handy."

"That's a wonderful idea. I'll go right up and see what's there. It'll give me a better idea of what's lacking."

"Indeed." She continued to regard her niece with a wary eye. "Of course, we may find out this whole scheme is impractical, you know. So I thought perhaps a trial run of, say, a month to six weeks. And, keep in mind, dear, you'll be taking on a lot. Should you decide to give up the plan later, I'll not fault you in any way."

Eliza's smile eclipsed the sun's brilliance. "I just can't thank you enough. I was afraid even to hope." She paused to draw breath, then continued in a rush, her words tumbling over themselves. "I realize it's going to cause some changes around here, but I promise to do my utmost to see that your life and your routine are affected as little as possible. You'll see."

"Yes, well, I assume we both will. In any event, you may take my tray now. And thank you for the lovely breakfast."

"You're ever so welcome. I'll be back to check on you soon." With the dazzling smile making her appear even younger than she was, she left the room.

Phoebe sank back against her pillows. "Dear Lord, I sure hope You know what You've gotten me into."

❧

Eliza could hardly wait to get started on the new project.

Working closely with Anabelle would be great fun—and not to be overlooked was the added bonus of keeping her own mind too busy to dwell on matters best ignored. With that thought, she headed for the enclosed staircase leading to the attic.

Not enough heat wafted from below to do much good in the steep-slanted top story of Harper House, she discovered upon ascending to its lofty heights. And in contrast to the warm sunshine, a brisk breeze whistled and howled around the structure's angles, adding an eerie quality to the venture. The cold made Eliza's teeth chatter as she stepped over a toppled dress form and picked her way through the dusty memorabilia of years gone by.

Arms crossed as she glanced around, Eliza debated going through any of the storage chests abutting one of the low walls. Undoubtedly they would contain outdated clothing, perhaps some seafaring mementoes that once belonged to Uncle Amos. And the old lamp standing dejectedly at the end of the row was not suitable for a child, nor would any of the paintings be, she was sure. Her captain uncle's tastes had leaned toward dark stormy seas, with stalwart vessels tossing among the churning waves.

But then her gaze fell upon the bedstead Aunt Phoebe had mentioned, and she stepped nearer to examine it more closely. Even under the coating of dust she recognized the rich cherrywood bed which had once graced her aunt's other guest room. As her fingers lightly traced the carved design in the wood, it brought back pleasant memories. She saw that the headboard and footboard were propped against each other, with the side pieces stacked neatly on the floor in front of them. There didn't seem to be a mattress anywhere in sight, but it couldn't take more than a few days to arrange for one. During that time, the room could be made ready. And against the far wall, she noticed, stood the matching wardrobe. Together the set was a wondrous find!

Tossing a cursory glance around the remainder of the

chilly area, she brushed her hands together and left for the stairs, decidedly elated over her good fortune.

"Well," Aunt Phoebe asked on her return, "did you come across anything you might be able to use?"

"Yes. As you said, the bedstead is there, along with the wardrobe. The two of them will be perfect."

She nodded. "Perhaps next time Micah comes by, we can prevail upon him to move those things down to the room for you."

"That would be marvelous. Well, I'd best wash the dust from my hands. It's time to open the shop."

It was all Eliza could do to keep her mind on business that afternoon, so taken was she in imagining a wallpaper pattern that would turn the dreary room into a charming haven and what type of yard goods to purchase for curtains. And she'd only just now thought of toys. At the very least there should be picture books and some dolls to cuddle, perhaps a miniature tea set.

It might do to have a ball and some toy soldiers, as well, though at the moment it seemed more prudent to plan for girls. With the likelihood of the Riccio sisters not being able to stay where they were for much longer, Eliza wanted to let Micah know there'd be a place where they would be looked after until permanent arrangements could be made.

"I say," the rather portly matron dressed entirely in black spoke up as she compared two lengths of handmade lace Eliza had given her to peruse. "Which of these would you say might look better used to accent the front of a shirtwaist?" She looked from one to the other and back, then peered up at Eliza.

"If it were up to me, I'd use the one in your left hand. It's just a touch heavier and would stand more wear."

"That's just what I was thinking," the older woman said with a smile. "I'll take both."

"Excellent. Will that be all?"

"Yes, miss. This is all I needed to finish my Christmas shopping." Handing money to Eliza, along with her choices, she meandered among the remaining displays while her purchases were wrapped. "I thank you," she said then, and with parcel in hand, she left.

Eliza checked the mantel clock and sighed. Closing time at last. She hoped Anabelle would come by soon to hear about Aunt Phoebe's decision.

"That should about do it, I'd say." Micah set down his end of the wardrobe he and his friend Charles Sprocket had lugged down from the attic. "How many trips up and down those stairs did this enterprise entail, anyway?"

The wiry redhead wiped his forehead on his sleeve and narrowed his gray eyes to a wince. "Between what we toted up there and what we brought back down to this room, must've been a dozen at least."

On the edge of his vision, Micah saw Anabelle jab an elbow into Eliza's ribs. "Would you listen to those poor, soft, overworked fellows. I never heard such moaning and groaning in my life."

"Nor have I," she agreed as she and Ana began wiping down the wood cabinet inside and out. "Why, Aunt Phoebe was quite set on doing the entire chore herself until I convinced her some strong, handsome gentlemen would make short work of it." She slanted Anabelle a merry glance, and they both giggled.

Charles straightened to his full, unimpressive height and puffed out his chest, which only strengthened the nasal quality of his jesting voice. "Strong as a bull, eh?"

The lad's more-than-interested glances toward Mrs. Harper's alluring niece were not lost on Micah. Obviously his friend was looking forward to escorting her to this evening's sacred concert. "Don't forget handsome," Micah quipped, trying to keep the mood easygoing. "She said 'handsome,' too." But the wink he'd intended for Ana ended up heading in Eliza's direction instead. In their bustling about, the two had somehow changed places. He felt his neck growing warm.

"In any event," Eliza said more seriously, not letting on if she'd noticed his mistake, "we thank you for your trouble. It's been a huge help."

"Seems like an awful lot to go through in wintertime for a mere bedroom," Charles remarked.

Micah tilted his head back and forth. "Oh, I don't know. Mrs. Harper likes company. Must be more relatives coming for the holidays."

At his comment, Anabelle and Eliza traded sly smiles and returned to their chore with renewed fervor.

Whatever this pair was up to, he decided, they seemed to be gaining a lot of enjoyment out of it. He hadn't seen Ana so lively and bubbly in ages. As for Eliza, well, she'd been unaccountably effervescent since Dr. Jenson pronounced her aunt well two days ago. Still, what Anabelle had mentioned regarding a sad loneliness being evident in Eliza's dusky blue eyes now seemed so obvious, Micah wondered why he'd missed noticing it before. He only hoped his redheaded pal treated the gently bred young woman with the respect she deserved.

Beside him, Charles brushed some lingering dust from his trousers and vest, tugging the latter back into proper position. Then he arched his golden brows. "Well, hard work gives a man an appetite. I'm starving."

"Don't fret," Anabelle answered. "Eliza's aunt is planning to serve us a light supper before we leave for the program."

"And we seem to be finished here," Eliza added. "The food must be ready by now."

❧

The fact that Micah's friend had come to lend a hand with the heavy furniture enabled Eliza to relax more than she normally would have in the presence of the virtual stranger. It also made it less awkward for her to agree to Anabelle's suggestion that they make a night of it, since one of the area's larger Presbyterian churches had scheduled a concert that evening.

By the time they arrived to enjoy the collection of hymns and carols rendered by organ, flute, and violin, she felt at ease, if not thrilled, at being in the company of the jovial bachelor. She wasn't quite ready to be escorted places by any young man but assured herself she could endure anything for a few hours. After all, she'd agreed to do this for Anabelle's sake.

Charles, she discovered not long into the program, had what appeared to be a nervous habit, in that he sniffed quite often. It hadn't been obvious at Aunt Phoebe's, as he'd been in and out of the room so much. But here in the quietness of the sanctuary, the intermittent sniffing stood out rather blatantly. Trying not to let on that she noticed, Eliza pretended to be looking the other way whenever he wiped his nose on a wrinkled handkerchief from his pocket. She almost wished he'd just blow the silly thing and be done with it. But the comical mental picture of him honking like a foghorn made her giggle inwardly.

"Something the matter?" Anabelle whispered from the other side of her.

Eliza shook her head and forced her attention toward the front, but it took awhile for her to completely compose herself, until well into the musical numbers.

After the program, the foursome went to a nearby coffeehouse called the Wooden Shoe. Each table was decorated in a Dutch motif with a red-and-white checked tablecloth and a vase containing red paper tulips, and Eliza noticed the menus were shaped like windmills. Only a few other tables were occupied when they entered, and those patrons gave them only casual glances as they passed.

Micah led their party to a quiet spot near the back of the establishment and seated Anabelle, while Charles pulled out Eliza's chair for her with exaggerated aplomb. "Your throne, milady."

"I thank you," she replied, elevating her eyebrows. His overt attentions merely encouraged her to maintain her distance from eager young bachelors in the future.

Within seconds, a waitress in Dutch attire took their orders for pie and coffee.

"That was a lovely concert," Anabelle remarked over their dessert. "They played some of my very favorites."

"And I noticed you paying particular interest to the woman at the organ," Eliza said.

"It's a habit of mine," she confessed.

"Well," Micah told her, "that young woman couldn't hold a candle to your talents, don't you agree, Eliza?" He flashed a warm smile.

Anabelle gave her no time to answer. She wrinkled her nose, her green eyes alight. "He always says the nicest things. Not always true, but nice, nonetheless."

Watching the interplay between them, Eliza wondered why they didn't sit closer to each other and why their little shows of affection seemed so few and far between. They almost gave the impression of being an old married couple rather than a man and woman deeply in love.

Well, it was no affair of hers, she told herself, and sampled another portion of her pie.

"Did you enjoy the ensemble's selection of musical numbers, Eliza?" Charles asked, his tone sincere.

"Yes, I thought it was a splendid program, especially the carol arrangements. I had a lovely time."

"Good. I was hoping perhaps you'd consider attending another similar concert with me two evenings hence."

She felt Micah's and Anabelle's eyes center on her. Eliza had told Ana before arranging this outing that she had no desire to begin keeping regular company with young men. Charles, it was true, had been the ultimate gentleman, and she really didn't want to encourage him. But neither did she wish to offend him. "Well, I—"

A shadow fell across their table as someone approached. "Why, Eliza!" a deep voice exclaimed. "What a surprise."

As her gaze swung up to that very familiar face, she felt all the color drain from her own. "W–Weston!" All but choking on the name, she sprang to her feet, toppling her chair in her haste. All thought vanished but one: escape.

fourteen

"Eliza! Wait!" Glaring at the intruder, who'd at least had the grace to step backward a pace, Micah jumped up and ran after her, barely acknowledging the astonished looks that passed between his fiancée and Charles Sprocket as he left them behind. He'd seen Eliza upset over her aunt's health, but never had he witnessed her turn white with shock and alarm as she'd done in this instance.

Nearing the door, he spied her warm cloak still hanging where they'd left their outerwear upon entering the restaurant. He plucked it from the hook on his way past and dashed out into the street.

Light snowflakes which had been floating and swirling on the night wind during the concert were now beginning to collect on the ground in a coating so thin it was almost transparent. But thankfully it was enough to indicate which direction Eliza had gone. In the flickering glow of the gaslights, he followed the small footprints around the next corner.

The sound of labored panting came from a darkened doorway of the second building, where he could see Eliza huddled in misery, pressing her hands to her cheeks, as if attempting to cool them.

She was turned slightly away, and at the sound of his footsteps, she let out a petrified scream. "Go away! Leave me alone!"

"Hey, it's all right," he crooned, stooping to draw her to her feet. "It's me. Micah."

She glanced beyond him, her eyes wide with fear. "D–don't make me go back there," she said between great gulps of air. "I don't want to face him."

"I'm not going to make you do anything you don't want to."

Compliant as a child, she allowed him to wrap her cloak about her shivering form. Then she began to cry.

Forgetting all but his concern for her, he pulled her close, cradling the back of her head as he rocked her in his arms. "Shh. You're safe now. No one's going to cause you harm. Come on, we'll see you home." Gently easing her away, he tucked her icy hand in the crook of his elbow and led her back to where they'd parked the buggy.

Anabelle and Charles exited the establishment as he was handing the still-distraught Eliza up into the upholstered backseat. He smiled with relief. "Sit with her, would you, Ana?" he asked quietly. "See what you can do."

She nodded, and when he helped her board, Anabelle took the spot next to Eliza, while the two men took the front seat. Draping an arm about Eliza, Ana hugged her close.

Until he had burst into her life again, Eliza had actually believed she was over the hurt and humiliation of being jilted by Weston Elliot. But the truth was that, for the most part, she had only suppressed her sadness and heartache. The few tears she'd cried in Aunt Phoebe's presence made her feel self-conscious, so she'd gathered the fragmented feelings together and pretended all was well. Yet running into her former betrothed here in New York was the last thing in the world she had ever expected.

Jostling homeward in Micah's buggy, Eliza felt her control gradually returning in the oppressive silence. But she knew her behavior in the Wooden Shoe had to have embarrassed her friends. Charles she cared little about, but what must Micah or Anabelle think of her? How would she ever hold her head up before them again?

Even as she pondered that heavy thought, she felt Ana give her an empathetic pat. Eliza raised her head and met her friend's concerned gaze. "I'm so very sorry. . . ." Her voice caught on a leftover sob. "I didn't mean to—"

Anabelle gave her an understanding smile. "Please; you mustn't apologize, Eliza. Whoever that cad was that he could upset you so, it most certainly is no fault of yours."

"But I spoiled the whole evening, and you must—"

"Pshaw! As I recall it, we were having the grandest of times up until that last moment. I'm just thankful you weren't alone."

So am I, Eliza vehemently agreed. *So am I.*

As it happened, Charles's house was the first they came to on the drive home. Upon reaching it, he hopped out. "Thanks, old man," he said with a smart salute to Micah and a reserved tip of the head toward Eliza and Anabelle. "Good evening, ladies. I rather enjoyed the concert. I trust you're feeling better, Eliza."

She nodded, but couldn't think of a suitable response. It was highly unlikely Charles Sprocket would ever venture within shouting distance of her again, she was certain of that. She just didn't care one way or the other right now.

When Micah at last pulled up before Harper House, he and Ana both alighted and helped Eliza down, then each took an arm to escort her up the walk.

"Thank you," she whispered. "But I can manage the rest of the way on my own. Truly."

"You're sure?" Anabelle prompted.

"Yes, perfectly. I'm fine. . .or will be, in time."

Ana continued to regard her. "Shall we postpone our shopping trip for a day or two?" she finally asked.

"No. Not at all. I'll be ready tomorrow at one, just as we planned. I promise." She added as much of a smile as she could manufacture.

"Well, watch your step," Micah urged. "The snow can be slick if you're not careful."

"I will; thank you." Eliza wanted to utter another heartfelt apology, but the kindness in their expressions would have been her undoing. She settled for something much simpler. "Good evening."

Her friends waited until she reached the door before driving off. Eliza waved and went inside. Finding the house quiet, she extinguished the downstairs lamps her aunt had left on for her, then trudged upstairs to give vent to the remainder of her anguish in private.

Awakening with the first streaks of dawn, Eliza snuggled deeper into the warmth of the blankets and quilts and once again thanked the Lord for getting her through the long night. Along with having emptied her soul of the last remnants of her tears, she had poured her heart out as well, ridding her being of the bitterness she'd been clinging to regarding Weston Elliot. It had taken that one glimpse of the man for her to realize the love she once felt for him was dead. He no longer had the power to hurt her.

With that final acceptance, a joyous peace flowed through her, filling all the secret corners inside. And now, by the grace of God, she knew she could face whatever lay ahead, be it the solitary life she'd found here with Aunt Phoebe or some other road of His choosing. All that mattered was that she be a vessel God could use to glorify His Son.

Gathering daylight had begun to creep between the folds of the window curtains, and Eliza pushed the covers aside so she could get up. She crossed to the washstand for the pitcher and basin and went downstairs for warm water.

Her aunt, always an early riser, was just coming from the kitchen with her own supply of water for her toilette.

"Good morning," they said in unison, then shared a smile as they parted company, each to prepare for the day.

When Eliza came down half an hour later, she found a breakfast of Aunt Phoebe's crepes and maple syrup waiting for her, a wonderful start for a busy morning.

By the time one o'clock arrived, and with it, Anabelle,

Eliza was eager to go shopping.

"You're looking surprisingly well," her friend remarked as she stood waiting for Eliza to don her wrap.

Aunt Phoebe turned to Eliza, unspoken questions in her eyes.

"Not to worry, Auntie," she said, slipping into her coat and gloves. "I crossed paths last evening with an old memory, but I'm over it now. I'll tell you all about it later. Right now, we have lots to do. Come on, Ana."

But once outside, Anabelle was not so easily put off. "You're quite certain that everything is well, Eliza? After your distress of last eve, I felt compelled to pray for you when I got home."

Eliza stepped near enough to hug her. "Which is likely one of the reasons why I've come to terms with it, dear friend. Thank you, from the bottom of my heart." Reaching the coach, she accepted the driver's help in boarding and gave him a grateful nod.

"Micah, too, was quite troubled over the whole affair," Anabelle went on, taking the seat opposite her as Graham flicked the lap robe over their legs. "I've scarcely seen him in such a black mood."

Eliza couldn't suppress a guilty sigh. "I feel rather awful that he had to come to my aid, yet I appreciated the fact that he did. Weston's sudden appearance caught me off guard. I'd thought that part of my life was past. I'll apologize to Micah next time I see him for his having dashed from your side like that just to rescue me."

"It's not necessary, really." Anabelle averted her attention to the passing buildings, and for a length of time, neither of them spoke.

Eliza finally broke the silence. "Weston Elliot, the man who approached me at the restaurant, was once my fiancé."

Her companion's green eyes turned to Eliza.

"Yes," Eliza continued before she used up her nerve.

"Shortly before our wedding was to take place, he ran off with my best friend." There. It was out. She'd actually said the words.

Anabelle's jaw dropped open. "You can't be serious. Why, no wonder it was a shock to see him again out of the blue."

With a nod of agreement, Eliza went on to confide the whole sordid affair. "So, as you might imagine," she said in conclusion, "I've been quite bitter at both of them for some time."

"And with good reason. Such nerve." Ana wagged her bonneted head.

"What's even more strange, however, is that I received word from my mother recently telling me that Melanie had returned home alone. She would speak to no one, but shut herself up in her old room. I didn't know what to make of it."

"Nor would I."

"In any event, last night I finally prostrated myself before God and turned over my misery and bitterness to Him. I didn't want to hold onto it for one more hour of my life. And He not only quite graciously took my burdens upon Himself like He promised, but He then filled me with the most incredible peace. I feel I can face anything now with Him beside me."

"Thank you, Eliza, for telling me all of this. I understand quite a lot of things now."

The carriage came to a halt in front of Macy's department store, and Graham again assisted the girls. "I'll be back for you in two hours, miss, to see if you've finished or need to be taken elsewhere."

"That will be fine. Thank you." Smiling, Anabelle reached for Eliza's hand, and the two of them hurried toward the entrance.

Eliza had been inside some elegant stores in her life, but none compared to this one for the fashionably attired patrons bustling about or the variety of merchandise available on every floor. Her gaze lost itself in festive displays reminding her of the approaching holiday season, but she was quick to remind herself that Christmas was not the primary reason for this shopping excursion.

By the time the allotted two hours drew to a close, they both had their arms filled with packages. "We couldn't possibly have forgotten anything, could we?" Eliza asked hopefully.

"Not that I can think of," Ana replied. "If it weren't for the fact that we must wait for delivery of the mattress, we could have the room set up for occupancy by this evening. But in the unlikely event we've overlooked something else that's crucial, we'll just schedule another shopping venture. I haven't had this much fun in ever so long."

"Neither have I. Won't Aunt Phoebe be amazed at all the practical and nice things we found for that room? I can't wait to show her."

Exiting the huge doors to the street outside, they spotted Graham waiting for them, and in no time at all, they were back at Harper House.

"I'm afraid I can't stay longer today," Anabelle confessed as she and her driver helped Eliza take all the purchases inside, "but I'll be back tomorrow morning. Perhaps between the two of us, we'll be able to make some progress in the room."

"I'll look forward to it. Thanks ever so much for coming with me today. It was grand to have your help, Ana."

As Eliza hung her wrap and watched the Dumonts' coach pull away and turn homeward, she heard Aunt Phoebe's step approaching her from behind.

"You have a visitor, dear. A tall gentleman, waiting for you in the sitting room. I was busy with customers when he first arrived, so I'm afraid I didn't get his name."

Instinctively, Eliza knew who it was. Her calmness amazed her, but she breathed a prayer for strength.

"Shall I make tea?"

"No, thank you, Auntie. I would appreciate it if you would come with me as I speak to him, however."

Though puzzled, Aunt Phoebe gave a consenting nod and moved to her side. "As you wish."

Eliza opened the French doors to the sitting room.

Weston got up immediately, dressed impeccably, as always. He'd grown a mustache, which somehow lengthened his face. "Eliza. Thank you for seeing me."

"Weston." She turned to her aunt. "Aunt Phoebe, this is Weston Elliot. I'm sure you've heard me mention his name."

"Yes." The older woman paled, yet remained nonplused as she glanced from the visitor to Eliza, then back again. "Mr. Elliot."

"Madam." He cleared his throat and sought Eliza's face. "Might we speak in private?"

"I think not. Whatever you have to say to me, you may say in front of my aunt." She motioned for the older woman to be seated, then took a chair near her. "Why have you come?"

A look of resignation crossed his chiseled features. Absently he toyed with the brim of his bowler, turning it around in his hands as his hazel eyes met hers.

"I hadn't planned to, actually, but when I happened to see you last night, I—" He glanced between them as if ill at ease, and his demeanor turned stony. "Confound it all, Eliza. I must speak to you alone."

Appalled that she had ever considered him handsome—or worse—compared him to a man as noble as Micah Richmond, Eliza hiked her chin. "I'm afraid that is not possible, Weston. You gave up that right some time ago. We have nothing further to discuss. I must ask you to leave now."

He studied her, as if expecting her to waver—as well she might have, in time past. When she did not, he expelled a huff of breath. "I'll go. For now. But not before I tell you what I came to say. I still love you, Eliza—"

Her incredulous gasp made no impression.

"And I shall be back. I want you to give us another chance."

Eliza turned to her aunt, her brows arched high. "Can you believe the man's gall, Auntie? Having cast me aside to dally with my bosom friend, he has now apparently done the same to Melanie, yet imagines I should take him back again, as if nothing untoward ever occurred between us."

Rising with measured dignity, he pursed his lips.

Was that anger she detected in that guarded expression?

"But I was a fool," came his placating explanation. "I see that now."

Even knowing what it cost a man like him to make that admission, Eliza held her ground. "Well, so was I, Weston, the worst kind of fool. But I'll not make that mistake again. It is over between us, now and forever. I have no desire to rekindle the cold ashes of an old fire. And I do not wish ever to lay eyes upon you again in this lifetime."

As she spoke, she watched a mutinous gleam rise in his eyes.

"I suggest you go back to your wife. Melanie could still be vulnerable to those questionable charms of yours."

His mustache quirked to one side. "I have no wife. I never married Melanie."

Eliza's mouth gaped in shock. "Then you are without a doubt the most despicable man I've ever had the misfortune to know. Get out of my sight, Weston Elliot. And do not come back here again. Ever."

A muscle worked in his jaw as he stared at her long and hard. But with little more than a flicker of a glance at her companion, he slapped his gloves against his palm, plunked his hat atop his obstinate head, and stalked away.

More than the bell rattled as the front door slammed shut behind him.

Eliza and her aunt sat stunned.

"Well," the older woman finally said, giving Eliza's knee an approving pat. "I assume that was the 'memory' you mentioned earlier."

"One and the same."

She chuckled. "I was never more proud of you, my dear. You showed the snake a lot of backbone."

"It was a gift from the Lord. Last night."

"Odd, though," Aunt Phoebe remarked. "He reminded me vaguely of someone."

Eliza laughed aloud. "I thought the same thing once, myself. But believe me, Auntie, I was entirely mistaken."

With a nod of agreement, she looked directly into Eliza's eyes. "And are you truly all right now?"

Smiling, she stood to help the dear woman to her feet. "I feel a bit like someone who just survived a battle, but it's comforting to be on the side that won. Do you suppose a cup of tea might be in order now, for a celebration?"

"I do, indeed."

But despite her brave show of force, Eliza couldn't help feeling sad for the girl who'd once been her cherished friend and whose life now was ruined. Silently she asked the Lord to heal Melanie Brown and to restore her self-respect.

fifteen

"Well, that's the end of it," Eliza said, stepping back to admire the last length of wallpaper she'd hung in place, its design one of charming forest animals frolicking amid groves of trees. "And not bad, for someone who's previously only watched the process from a safe distance, I might add." She leveled a glance at Anabelle, seeking her approval.

Her friend, though decidedly less than keen on messing with gummy paste or sloppy brushes, had made a valiant attempt at lending a hand. She appeared almost as disheveled as Eliza felt. "I'd say it looks. . .sufficiently. . .childlike."

Sputtering into a giggle, Eliza turned her eyes heavenward. "Are you telling me it resembles the work of a child?"

"No, not at all." Ana pinkened delicately. "What I meant was it should appeal to one."

"Oh, well that's better. Then let's clean up the rest of this clutter so we can go down for a bite of dinner. You must be just as hungry as I am, after all this hard work."

Already gathering remnants of discarded wall covering together in a somewhat neat pile, Anabelle straightened and assessed the room. "When the mattress is delivered and we make up the bed, it should be quite homey in here."

"Especially after I finish hemming the curtains and put them up," Eliza added. "I truly appreciate your help, Ana."

"I'm amazed we've been able to accomplish so much in only a few days."

"Well, I just hope it's soon enough." She swung dreamily around in a circle, her arms wide. "Oh, can't you just picture a little girl or two, coming here from a shabby hovel where people have been crowded together like cattle? Imagine how it'll feel to realize there'll be only one other person in this huge bed, in a clean room with pretty colors and lots of new playthings. . ."

The honey blond tilted her head back and forth, her demeanor unreadable.

"Of course, I know this whole effort might be for naught," Eliza continued as she resumed tidying up. "It could turn out that there are suddenly enough beds at other shelters. Maybe there won't be a need for one more place, temporary or otherwise. But just knowing that if one arises, we do have a suitable room should make this all worthwhile. And won't it be fun seeing the expression on Micah's face when he finds out what we've done?"

"He's sure to be surprised. It's been hard not confessing why I've been spending so much time with you these past few days." A wistful smile lit Ana's features. "But here I've been, deriving pleasure from merely decorating a bedroom, while you've been thinking ahead to its occupants, to helping those he carries such a burden for. I. . .sometimes wish I could feel as strongly as he does about them. As strongly as you seem to."

Eliza knew the young woman had spoken candidly, and though she had almost as hard a time understanding how someone could *not* care about the hopeless predicament faced by so many immigrants, she did not feel it was her place to judge. "You do what you can in contributions and your sewing. Everything helps, believe me."

"Perhaps." She paused, as if trying to formulate her next comment. When she spoke again, her voice was subdued. "But I often wonder if I will ever truly be the wife Micah needs."

Setting aside the refuse she had gathered, Eliza crossed the room to give her an encouraging hug. "Don't be silly. You two have loved each other forever. And that's what's most important in a marriage."

"Is it?" Anabelle asked quietly, drawing away. "Then, why haven't we *been* married forever already? Most of our friends have made that commitment and are now in the throes of parenthood, raising broods of children. Micah and I, on the other hand, merely see each other every day—or almost every day. And instead of growing closer, we're almost—"

She waved a hand uselessly before her face. "Oh, never mind. I shouldn't bother you with our problems."

"That's what friends are for, is it not?" Eliza answered gently. "Personally, I feel your concerns are completely ungrounded, and that in time, you two will work out your differences and get married. See if you don't."

But Anabelle didn't seem overly comforted by Eliza's assurance. She just bent down and picked up some of the trash.

❧

Making a hasty loop of the horse's reins at the hitching post in front of the Dumont house, Micah all but ran up the walk. He paused at the door to straighten his coat sleeves and catch his breath, then rapped.

In seconds, Anabelle swung the portal wide and stepped out of the way so he could enter. "We thought you weren't coming. We've already started without you."

"I'm truly sorry I'm late, sweetheart, but I'm afraid it couldn't be avoided." Removing his gloves, hat, and coat, he disposed of them on the hall tree.

"Let me guess," she challenged in syrupy tones, arms crossed as she eyed him with irritation. "Some destitute family needed groceries, and there's no one on Earth who can see they get some but you. Or yet another street urchin out in the cold, with no place to go until you happened by. Or—"

Clasping her upper arms, Micah looked directly into her eyes, the gray-green depths decidedly cooler than normal. He tempered the tone of his voice, not wanting to speak harshly to her, yet pronouncing the words slowly and distinctly. "It's what I do, Ana. I go where there's a need, wherever and whenever I must. You know that. You've always known it."

She pressed her lips into a thin line and stared for a few seconds before relenting. "Yes, I know. It's just—I get so tired of waiting for you, never knowing if you'll be on time, or late, or even come at all. And Mother and Papa are forever asking when they might start plans for the wedding, and. . ."

Drawing her close, Micah hugged her. "I understand, sweetheart, I really do. And I wish I could make things easier for you. I just don't know how."

"Yes, you do," she insisted, her cheek against his chest. "You could find some other employment. There are lots of other ways one can help people. In fact, Papa told me there's an opening at the bank for someone with your qualifications. You'd be able to arrange financial aid for the unfortunates."

"Ana, I—"

"Are you coming to the table, Daughter?" came her father's voice from the dining room.

"Yes, Papa. We'll be right there." Releasing a weary breath, she stepped out of Micah's embrace and took his arm. "Come on; we always set a place for you, regardless."

In the face of the false smile she'd plastered on, he hesitated.

She gave another tug, a trifle more playful this time.

He still didn't move. He could see she was in a mood, one that had been coming on for some time. Well, so was he, and he was getting rather tired of always defending his calling. "Now and then I wish you'd be just a little more understanding," he heard himself say, the words coming out before he could stop them. "I've had a beastly day today. Nothing worked out right, no matter what I tried. Everywhere I turn there's more need than I can alleviate—"

"Need, need, need," she wailed, rocking back on her heels, bright circles of color rising on her cheeks. "Honestly, between you and Eliza, I hear more than I can bear about poor people and homeless children and the miserable, huddled masses. Why don't you two put your heads together and come up with some grand plan or noble scheme that'll solve all the problems of mankind! Obviously she suits you more than I ever will."

"What?" Flabbergasted at the uncharacteristic outburst, Micah could only gape at her.

"Anabelle!" From the dining room a chair scraped back.

"Supper's getting cold," she muttered through clenched teeth.

"Well, I thank you for the invitation," he said, rising anger throbbing through him with each beat of his heart, "but I find I have no appetite after all." Crossing to the hall tree, he put on his coat. "Good night."

"Oh, Micah. . ." Her tone turned apologetic.

Past caring, and not even bothering to close the door after himself, Micah strode purposefully to his buggy, yanking the reins free on his way to the seat. He clucked his tongue and slapped the traces against the horse's back without so much as a backward glance.

In his room a short while later, he kneaded his jaw, forcing himself to relax those muscles. Now that he'd calmed down, he wasn't really angry with Anabelle so much as disappointed. And at the end of his patience. How could it be that despite all his efforts and a virtual mountain of fervent prayers, his fiancée was no closer to accepting his ministry, but in fact seemed to be drifting farther from it? Why couldn't she be more like—

Without permitting his wayward mind to complete the comparison, he sank to his knees. He was done in, mentally and physically, and knew he lacked whatever it took to deal with disillusionment right now. He needed a new supply of wisdom and strength. . .the kind he could obtain only from spending time with his Lord.

❧

"Hm. I wonder why Anabelle hasn't come today?" Eliza

mused, checking out the window for the dozenth time. The pale afternoon sun was well on its downward slide, lengthening the shadows of the hemlock trees.

Aunt Phoebe set down the crystal vase she'd been dusting and turned. "Well, it is quilting day. Perhaps she was needed at the sewing circle, for a change."

"I'm sure that must be it. I have rather been taking over her every spare moment lately. I just surmised that with the mattress due to be delivered this afternoon, she'd have wanted to be here to help me make up the bed with the lovely variegated green counterpane she helped pick out."

"I wouldn't worry about it, dear. No doubt she'll come by tomorrow."

Crossing to the chair to put the final stitches into a pair of soft green and white curtains, Eliza retook her seat. "I suppose you're right, Auntie." *But surely Ana would have mentioned something about having another engagement,* Eliza told herself.

Her unease multiplied a short time later, when she looked up from counting the number of lace scarves remaining in one of the gift shop cabinets, to see Micah Richmond entering the room.

"Oh, yes, the contribution," Aunt Phoebe said as he approached the counter.

"I know it's not my usual day, ladies," he said cheerily, "but I was in the neighborhood." He glanced around in curiosity. "Ana's not here?"

Eliza shook her head. "Her talents must have been needed at church. I've been monopolizing the poor girl far too much these days."

"Strange; I just came from there. When I stopped by to see if they'd finished any new quilts, everyone started hounding me with questions, wondering why she hasn't been coming lately."

Prickles of alarm skittered down Eliza's back. "Weren't

you with her last night? Did she mention having other plans or anything?"

Tugging at his cravat, he cleared his throat. "I. . .uh. . .did go there for supper, actually. Couldn't stay long, though. She didn't say much."

"How odd," Aunt Phoebe murmured. "Now I'm beginning to worry about the dear girl myself."

"Well, put your minds at ease, my friends," Micah said with assurance. "I'll call on her this evening and find out if anything's amiss. Perhaps she's had one of her headaches and wanted to rest at home."

"Of course," the older woman said, sounding somewhat encouraged.

"Be sure to give her our love," Eliza added. "And tell her we missed her smiley face around here."

"I'll do that." With a grin, he turned for the door.

"Wait, son. I've yet to give you my contribution," Aunt Phoebe said.

Halting, he swung around, chagrined. "Oh, yes. I must be a touch overtired myself." Accepting the funds she held out to him, he left.

Eliza didn't know how long she continued to watch after him, but when she caught herself staring into nothingness, she sent a silent prayer aloft for Anabelle.

❧

It took considerable courage for Micah to approach his fiancée's home that evening, considering his hasty and heated departure the previous night. But after so many people had asked about her during the day, he was concerned. Tying the horse at the rail, he strode up to the door and knocked.

Anabelle's mother answered the summons. "Oh. Micah. I wasn't expecting you." Ever dignified and proper, every graying brown hair on her queenly head in place, there came no typical smile to soften the timeless beauty of her face. But the familiar countenance seemed no less friendly, despite a few added lines around her green eyes—eyes that were lightly rimmed in red at the moment.

"I wasn't coming for supper, Mother Dumont. I was wondering if I might speak with Ana."

Nibbling the corner of her lip, she shifted from one foot to the other, as if hesitating to answer at first. "I'm afraid she isn't available just now."

"To anyone," he asked, "or just to me?"

Another slight hesitation. "She asked me to give you something. Wait just a moment." Withdrawing from the immediate vicinity of the door, she returned directly, a sealed envelope in her hand. "I hope this will answer your questions. I—" A mist rose in her eyes, and she closed them momentarily while she swallowed. "Good evening, Micah."

Ana's letter clutched in his hand, he watched as the door closed gently in his face, leaving him little choice but to go home.

sixteen

Micah lingered on the Dumonts' doorstep for a long moment, debating whether to knock again and hope Anabelle would come to the door this time. Or if she didn't, perhaps her mother would go into a few more details. It was quite obvious the woman had been crying. What had upset her?

But considering the close relationship he had always enjoyed with Ana's parents, Mother Dumont wouldn't have hesitated to invite him inside—or at the very least, answer the question he'd put to her—unless something was very, very wrong.

Releasing a pent-up breath, he slid the letter she had given him into an inside pocket and walked back to his buggy. Then he took the shortest route back to Columbus Avenue and made quick work of stabling the horse and parking the buggy before going into his room.

The place was cool from being vacant and shut up all day, but the temperature didn't faze him as he tossed his coat and hat onto the arm of the sofa. More for light than heat, he lit the logs he routinely laid in the fireplace each morning, then lit the lamp next to his overstuffed chair and sank wearily to the seat. In seconds he had Ana's letter open:

My dearest Micah,

After the way I spoke to you when we were last together, I felt horrid. To think you and I would ever come to the place where we could actually say hurtful things to each other dealt me a crushing blow. Knowing you as I do, you must have felt the same.

Be that as it may, I cannot help but believe we were

honest in expressing our innermost feelings. Perhaps more truthful than we have ever been before.

"Were we, Anabelle? We barely discussed anything. There wasn't time to really talk." Shifting in his chair, Micah focused again on the neatly penned missive:

But there were important things which I, for one, left unsaid. I will try to write them as best I can now.

I think I have always loved you. Whether that fact can be attributed to the long-standing relationship shared by our parents, or perhaps even came to be because of it, I cannot be sure. Certainly knowing their grand expectations for us had to have played some part in our planning to marry one day.

Micah, despite himself, had to agree with that statement, at least to some extent. Yet there'd never been anyone else—for either of them. Didn't that prove something? Impatiently he looked back at the letter:

I doubt it is possible to completely analyze the deep affection I feel for you. You have been my best friend, my confidant, at times even a big brother, offering whatever I needed, always giving the best of yourself. You could give no less, for that is the kind of man you are.

I am, and have always been, very proud of you, Micah. It has been with great joy and wonder that I watched you turn from a freckle-faced lad who delighted in putting frogs in my pocket, to a handsome champion of the downtrodden. The Lord has blessed you with that kind of generous and unselfish nature, and in my heart I know He has wonderful things in store for you.

However, I have recently come to realize that those plans do not include me.

"You can't mean that, Ana. We've always planned to marry one day. There's no reason we couldn't. Or shouldn't. We'd be throwing away a lifetime of caring." Emitting a ragged breath, he read on:

Looking around at so many of our closest friends and their marriages, I cannot help but see that for a marriage to endure there must be a certain kind of harmony. And though you and I possess that in some ways, it is sadly lacking in the most important one. Try as I might, I cannot force myself to enter into that benevolent work you feel is your ministry.

"No, you're wrong. You just need time. Time, and maybe an opportunity to come with me on my calls, to see things with your own eyes. It would make a difference."

For that reason, I have decided to leave New York for an undetermined period.

Micah slammed a palm against the armrest of his chair. Where would she have gone?

I have petitioned my parents not to divulge my whereabouts. We need an opportunity to be apart from each other and seek the will of the Lord in regards to our future.

At this, he crumpled the pages in his hands and lay his head back, staring at the ceiling. A deep emptiness surged through him, one so profound he could hardly bring himself to read farther. But finally the need to know the rest made him unravel the letter and smooth out the wrinkles as best he could.

Meanwhile, I pray you will not cease your efforts concerning the immigrants for whom you carry such a heavy burden. I will think of you charging off to their rescue each morning. I draw great comfort from knowing that others, like Eliza, share that call. Through my friendship with her, I came as close as I ever could to actually entering into your ministry. Truly, her heart is as big as yours. The two of you would make a wonderful team. And should it grow beyond that, one day, I should hold no ill feelings against either of my two very dearest friends.

Please don't forget me, dearest Micah, for you will always be in my most fervent prayers.

With deepest love,
Anabelle

Utterly stunned, Micah could neither think nor pray. There'd never been a time in his life when Ana hadn't been there for him. True, they'd drifted somewhat apart when he began working with Child Placement, but he'd always envisioned their relationship eventually deepening to include that.

But this. This sounded so final, as if she had already thought about it and prayed about it and come to this irrevocable conclusion. She would go her way; he would go his. It wasn't supposed to happen like this.

Was it?

❧

Morning dawned hours later than usual, Micah was sure of that. Not having slept at all during the longest night of his life, the first streaks of daylight found him still in his clothes in the upholstered chair.

All too soon he'd have to leave for work.

Have to go about this day as if nothing unusual had occurred.

Have to get involved with other people's troubles and struggles with the same fervor he'd always shown.

His spirit was too heavy to pray. He'd tried, heaven knew he'd tried, but no words would come. And now as he sat listless and lifeless, he wondered how many days and nights would pass before he became accustomed to existing without the one person who'd made up almost the entire other half of his world.

Releasing all the air from his lungs in a whoosh, he dragged himself up and headed for his shaving brush and razor. And he hoped for all he was worth that there wouldn't be some huge problem to deal with today.

❧

Eliza tucked the sheets around the mattress in the newly outfitted guest room, then added a blanket and counterpane before fluffing the pillows. She felt guilty that she hadn't waited for Anabelle, but there'd been no word of her friend as yet.

Moving to the wardrobe, she assessed its contents. Ana's parents, upon hearing of the venture, had contributed generously toward a variety of simple nightwear and everyday clothing and underthings to keep in store, plus several kinds and sizes of shoes for young children of either gender. But Eliza's first thoughts continued to center on the little Riccio girls, whose plight had inspired this action on her part. Somehow it seemed only right if they turned out to be the first occupants of this small haven.

She stepped to the doorway and swung a critical glance about. It was as ready as it ever would be.

It was nearing suppertime when Micah at last made an appearance. Something in the sag of his shoulders, the lack of the usual twinkle in his eye, signaled dire news. Eliza observed a peculiar tightness in his expression and new lines of strain, particularly around his mouth. It almost seemed an effort for him to smile.

Aunt Phoebe, obviously having drawn the same conclusions, spoke up first. "My. It would appear this has not been the best of days. Is something amiss?"

He drew his lips into a grim line. "I've had better."

"Well, sit right down, lad. We were just about to partake of supper, but there's plenty. If you've no other plans, perhaps you'd be interested in joining us, for a change—unless you're expected elsewhere."

His nod of acceptance seemed to indicate a slight improvement in spirit. "If you don't think you'll find me depressing company. As it turns out, I do happen to be on my own tonight."

"Not at all," she assured him. "It'll be a rare treat for my niece and me. We get weary of only having each other to look at across a table." Waving him to the nearest chair, she turned to Eliza. "Bring the man some tea, will you, dear? And I'll check on our meal."

Hurrying to do her aunt's bidding, Eliza couldn't help wondering why Micah wouldn't be supping with the Dumonts, as was his custom. Whatever the reason, though, it truly would be nice to have someone to talk to over supper besides her aged relative. She poured a cup of strong tea and took it to the parlor. "Do you take sugar? Cream?" she asked, handing him the drink.

Warmth returned to his eyes when he smiled. "Cream sometimes, but black will do. Thanks."

"Supper will be ready shortly. Just sit here and relax." At his nod, she returned to the kitchen.

Over succulent roast chicken and buttered potatoes a little while later, Aunt Phoebe managed to keep the conversation centered around pleasantries while Micah gradually lost much of his somberness. And when at last he started appearing more himself, she finally broached the earlier topic. "So, you mentioned you were having a horrid day before you came to us."

He nodded grimly, but now, at least, with some of the old optimism.

"Bad news from the Garibaldis?" Eliza probed, her pulse quickening as she anticipated his surprised pleasure upon discovering her and Anabelle's secret awaiting upstairs.

"It's partly that, yes. I'm afraid it's as we feared. The couple finds it impossible to continue providing for their friends' orphaned daughters. They need to be relieved of the burden immediately. And I'm out of options. There's just no place to put them."

"Oh, but there is," Eliza blurted out.

He looked up, as if suddenly seeing her for the first time.

"It was a surprise. Anabelle and I have been working on it for days."

Some of the customary ruddiness in his complexion paled. He cleared his throat. "What do you mean?"

Eliza sought her aunt's approving nod and took heart. "That guest room you and Charles carried furniture into—well—Aunt Phoebe has allowed me to furnish it to be used as a shelter for children. Whenever you find you have one or two little ones who have absolutely nowhere else to go, we can put them up, temporarily, until more permanent arrangements can be made."

"You're not joking?"

"Of course not, silly. And it would thrill me no end to be able to look after little Rosa and Gabriella while you find them a new home. However long it takes."

He shook his head in wonder. "I am speechless. Never in a million years would I have imagined something like this."

"Would you care to see it?"

Looking from Eliza to her aunt and back again, Micah blotted his mouth on his napkin and stood. "Lead the way, dear girl. Lead the way."

She smiled and impulsively snatched him by the hand, grabbing a lantern from the hallway on their way to the staircase. Then she all but raced up the steps with him in tow. Nibbling her lip in anticipation, she flung the door wide and gestured for him to enter. She held the lantern high.

"Look at this," he said in awe, stepping inside, his words

carrying a tone of incredulity. He surveyed the new quarters momentarily, then turned to search her face. "And this was all your idea, I take it?"

Nodding, Eliza felt a blush warming her cheeks. "But Aunt Phoebe had some good suggestions, and of course, Anabelle helped me pick things out, plus did half the work. We could hardly keep from telling you! And her parents, the Dumonts, gave us money to buy some children's clothing. What do you think?"

"What do I think?" He scratched his head, still displaying overwhelming surprise. "I'm deeply touched, Eliza. More so than I can express. I felt on the verge of complete hopelessness when I arrived at your door this eve, yet now, I—" He turned to glance once more into the room, bracing a hand on the doorjamb as he took everything in.

Eliza, deeply moved at Micah's inability to express his feelings, stayed her tears. "I only wish Anabelle had come with you," she murmured. "It was as much her surprise as it was mine. She should have been in on your reaction, too."

Micah's back was to her at the moment, and she saw him stiffen, heard the ragged intake of breath. His palm slid down the wooden frame. "She. . .uh. . .is gone, Eliza."

"Gone?" she echoed, the pitch of her voice high in disbelief. "What do you mean, gone?"

"Just that." He turned, placing both hands on her shoulders as he looked straight into her eyes. "Anabelle has left New York—for good, apparently—and I haven't a clue where she is."

seventeen

Eliza gawked at Micah for a full minute, aghast. "You can't be serious! Anabelle, gone? How can that be possible? I don't believe it. I won't."

"Believe it or not, it's your choice," he said resignedly. "Nevertheless, she has left New York, for who knows where. Mother Dumont would give me no information, I can't think of any distant relatives. Nothing."

"And she led you to assume she won't be coming back?"

"Quite."

Becoming aware of a throbbing in her temples, Eliza drifted to the top landing and sank onto it, setting the lantern on the floor while she cupped her head. Then she looked back up at him, his features heavily shadowed in the subdued light. "But why? What possible reason could Ana have had for simply vanishing from us so suddenly? She never even hinted she was unhappy. Oh, this is all too much."

Micah eased down beside her and rested his elbows on his thighs, his hands dangling between his knees as he stared straight ahead. "I couldn't have put it better myself."

"But didn't she say anything to you? Give any warning at all?" It was so reminiscent of when Weston and Melanie disappeared out of the blue.

He shook his head.

Eyeing him, Eliza sensed he knew more than he was telling her. "And she left no word whatsoever?"

He winced. "A letter. Her mother gave it to me last night."

"Well at least that's something, is it not? What did Ana say? If you don't mind my asking, of course."

"It's a long story, Eliza. I'm not sure I can go into it all just yet. I'm still having problems enough dealing with it as it is."

"Oh, do forgive me. I'm sure it must have been quite personal." She paused. "There wasn't. . .I mean, it wasn't. . .well, surely no other man was involved." The very idea made Eliza cringe.

"Not to my knowledge, no."

"That's comforting, at least."

Micah gave a little huff. "Small comfort, I'd say."

"Of course. I'm sorry, Micah, really I am. This is just so unexpected. I can't quite figure out what to make of it. I can't even think."

He tilted his head and opened his mouth as if about to ask something, then closed it again.

"What is it?"

Studying his hand as he flexed and unflexed it, he finally turned to Eliza but then couldn't hold her gaze. "I don't suppose. . .that is, did she ever express any doubts to you. . . concerning our engagement?"

Eliza searched back in her memory, trying to dredge up every last word Anabelle had said during the times they'd been together. "I know she loves you very much and has done so most of her life. But she did wonder aloud, once, if she'd ever be the sort of wife you needed."

"That's what she wrote in the letter, too," he admitted miserably. "Utterly ridiculous, really—especially since her doubts seem connected primarily to my work. But any misgivings she might have had she should have discussed with me. And we could have worked them out together."

Eliza could only nod in agreement.

"Well," he said at length, "it seems neither of us has much light to shed on the situation. At least, not enough to make her action seem even remotely practical." He got up and offered a hand. "I do thank you for the listening ear, anyway. You're about the closest friend I've got at the moment."

Placing her fingers into his, Eliza shook her head as she

rose, grasping the lantern on her way. "Considering what becomes of my 'best friends,' " she muttered dryly as they slowly descended, "I wouldn't count your association with me much of an asset."

He chuckled under his breath. "Nevertheless, we're all each other seems to have at the moment. And we may appreciate knowing there's one person with whom we feel free to unburden our souls."

Eliza found that statement oddly comforting.

"Speaking of burdens," he said as they reached the bottom, "might I assume your problem of the other evening has worked itself out?"

Another maddening blush did its best to appear. "Yes. After considerable prayer and submission to the Lord's will, the matter is ended. That particular man won't bother me again."

"Good. Ana and I prayed for you when we parted that night."

"Thank you. I—"

"Oh, there you two are," Aunt Phoebe said, breezing toward them. "I've cleared the table of the meal, made a pot of fresh coffee, and am about to serve dessert, if anyone's interested."

"Sounds good to me," Micah said pleasantly.

Eliza only smiled, and they gathered around the table once again.

"What did you think of the new guest room upstairs?" the older woman asked, slicing a generous hunk of chocolate cake and passing it to their guest.

"Most amazing. I had absolutely no idea the ladies had undertaken such a marvelous project. Eliza tells me you're in agreement to my bringing a child or two here on occasion, to be looked after temporarily?"

She nodded and served the next piece to Eliza. "I did have a few reservations about the matter, but my niece assures me she will manage the venture adequately."

"Well," Micah replied, "it would appear you'll be having your first young visitors tomorrow. I can't say for how long they'll need lodging, but I will be doing my utmost to find them a permanent family."

"We'll be ready," Eliza said. But the excitement she had expected to feel was tempered now with the sad news of Anabelle's absence.

❧

Loading the meager bundle of his young charges' belongings into the buggy before heading back inside, Micah drew a fortifying breath and prayed for strength to get the children through yet another wrenching parting. Even before the Garibaldis' doorway came into view, he could hear wailing and sobbing echoing the length of the dreary hallway. A few curious heads peeked out of other apartments lining the corridor.

"Dere, dere, bambinos," the overwrought woman of the household crooned soothingly as he approached. "Nice'a Mr. Richmond, he finda you a new mama, new papa. Everyt'inga be better, eh?"

"N–no, no," Gabriella sobbed, clinging to her guardian's legs with the dogged strength of a six-year-old. "We s–staya here. Wit you."

Tiny Rosa, smothered protectively in a tangle of other dark-eyed children's arms, peered between them from a few feet away, her doe eyes huge with fear.

By now even the lady herself had to blot tears on her apron as she looked hopelessly to Micah, then patted the little girl's head. "It'a be better. You see. We come'a visit sometime."

"No, Mama," Vinnie whined, confusion drawing his boyish eyebrows into a vee above his nose as he huddled over Rosa. "Dey can have my food. Don'a make'a dem go. Please, no."

But in a show of sheer determination, she peeled Gabriella's thin arms from around herself and shoved her forcibly to Micah. "It'sa for da best. You see. Better nobody starve."

Trying his utmost to hang onto the distraught, weeping little girl even now twisting to get out of his clutches, Micah watched Mrs. Garibaldi extract the younger sister from her own children's embrace and deposit the toddler in his free arm. Then, somehow managing to corral her own little ones behind one deceptively strong arm and leg, she closed the door with her other hand, and the wailing on that side diminished by half.

Gabriella's, however, went up a few notches. "No! No! Don'a take us awa–a–y–y–y." Using all her energy now in a last desperate attempt to squirm free, she slipped low enough to give a mighty kick to her abductor's shin.

Micah saw stars as the searing pain shot up his entire leg but grasped the girls even harder, limping the remaining distance to the buggy.

To alleviate the damp chill of the day, he'd draped a quilt open on the seat beside his place. Depositing the children onto it, he held them in place while making swift work of wrapping the bulky lengths around the pair.

Gabriella, though still crying audibly, appeared to recognize her inevitable defeat. The sobs turned to coughs, and she went rigid, sitting stiff as a board while Micah tucked the free ends under her and her sister's slight weight. Rosa's bewilderment led only to whimpers as she huddled close to her sibling.

Fairly confident that he was winning, Micah gulped a huge breath and climbed aboard, clucking the horse into motion. He knew better than to count the victory prematurely, though, and sought assistance from the Lover of all children even as he pulled out onto the thoroughfare.

During the long drive to Harper House, he kept up a running dialogue in the quiet tones of a confidant. "I know you'll like the nice room where you'll be spending the night. Some of my real good friends have fixed it up especially for you. These ladies love children, but God never gave them any of their own, so they just help little ones whenever they can. They'll have plenty of good food and even some things for you to play with all the time you're there. I expect you to remember the manners your mama and Mrs. Garibaldi taught you and be on your best behavior."

Beside him, Gabriella hunched deeper into the confining folds of patchwork squares, leftover sobs still racking her spindly form. She stared miserably in the direction of her shrouded feet but didn't respond.

His own heart melting over their despair, Micah's prayers turned to petitions for Eliza and Mrs. Harper, that the Lord would provide wisdom, grace, and fortitude beyond all their expectations.

When they finally neared the wide panorama of the Hudson, its waves sparkling up ahead, he turned the bay toward Harper House, circling around to the back door. He felt Gabriella brace herself as he drew to a stop. "We're here, girls. Let me help you down."

As if all the spirit had drained out of her, the six-year-old offered no resistance when Micah unwrapped the quilt and set her and her sister onto the ground. Then, tucking their bundle under one arm, he took their hands on either side of him and led them up the walk.

A tapered finger parted the curtain, and Eliza met his gaze with a tentative smile before opening the door. She stooped down to the level of the little newcomers, but wisely maintained her distance since the pair had been sleeping the only time she'd been in their presence. "Well, who have we here?"

"This is Gabriella Riccio," he said, tipping his head first at one, then at the other, "and her sister, Rosa. Girls, I'd like you to meet Miss Eliza. She'll be looking after you for a while."

This time, the sad-eyed youngsters shrank imperceptibly back against Micah's legs, Rosa's inconsequential weight aggravating the knot which had already formed on his shin. He nudged them gently inside, two tiny hands tightening their grip on his.

"I hope those cookies are for us," he said brightly, nodding toward the kitchen table, where a heaping plate of cookies and sliced apples sat next to a pitcher of milk. "That ride made us pretty hungry." Bending over, he helped the two off with their threadbare coats.

Eliza smiled and hung the wraps on the wall pegs. "They sure are. Auntie Phoebe and I baked them while we were waiting for you."

The young faces brightened a measure.

As if suddenly hearing her name, the older woman entered the kitchen, beaming from ear to ear. "Well, well, well. I see our visitors have arrived."

"This is my aunt, children," Eliza said. "You may call her Auntie Phoebe or Mrs. Harper, whichever you wish."

But four yearning brown eyes were already devouring the treats in view.

"I'd say there are some hungry tummies around here," Micah piped in. "Come to the table, girls." He ushered them across the room, helping them onto chairs. Taking a seat next to Gabriella, while Eliza chose the one by Rosa, he bowed his head. "We thank You, dear Lord, for Miss Eliza and Aunt Phoebe's kindness in providing some good food and a nice place for Gabriella and Rosa to stay. Please bless them all. In Jesus' name, amen."

The children crossed themselves and centered their attention on the fruit and cookies, while Mrs. Harper brought glasses to the table and filled them with milk.

Picking up the plate, Eliza removed a cookie and slice of apple for herself, then offered some to Rosa.

When the youngster shyly met her gaze and warm smile, she hesitantly took one of each, immediately biting a chunk of apple, and Eliza passed the dish to Gabriella.

"I'm going to have two of each," came Micah's loud whisper and conspiratorial wink from her other side. "You may, too, if you like."

"Graci." She sighed and helped herself, but snatched another cookie and apple slice for her sister before relinquishing the plate.

"Did you see any pretty sights on the drive?" Eliza asked between bites. "There are so many lovely decorations up for Christmas."

Munching her cookie, Gabriella shook her head.

"Well, I sure did," Micah said pleasantly. "But I think what the girls would really like to see is the nice bed where they'll be sleeping later this evening."

"D–dis'a where you live'a too?" Gabriella asked him, her voice wavering.

"No, but I come by quite often to see my friends, so I'll be checking in on you and Rosa a lot."

That seemed to pacify her for the moment.

Micah took that as an encouraging sign. At least there wouldn't be another dreadful scene at bedtime—hopefully. He glanced at Eliza, awed by the love in those blue eyes as she gazed at the girls the Lord had sent her. *Too bad Anabelle could never find it within herself to be that way,* he thought with a bittersweet pang. But that was something he might as well accept.

Eliza looked up at him just then, nibbling her lower lip the way she did whenever she felt a little nervous. He grinned at her. The Lord knew what He was doing when He'd put thoughts of this undertaking into that pretty head. Micah had no doubt about that. And he knew somehow that it wouldn't take Gabriella and Rosa long to settle in.

Too bad it couldn't be forever.

eighteen

Eliza was extremely grateful that Micah hung around for awhile, chatting casually with her and Aunt Phoebe, including the children now and then in the conversation. Soon enough, the older woman heard a summons to go attend the shop. And by the time the rest had finished the refreshments, Gabriella seemed a little more at ease, if not thrilled about her fate. Rosa had yet to utter a word, but stared intently at Eliza with childlike candor. Eliza wondered if the sprite even knew how to talk.

As she watched the somber expressions on the youngsters gradually softening, she ventured a suggestion. "Would you like to go upstairs and see your room?"

The older one slid a furtive glance toward Micah, as if looking for his approval. . .or perhaps wondering if this was when he, too, would go away, leaving her and her sister with these near strangers.

"I say," he answered, ruffling her dull, stringy curls, "that's a wonderful idea." Getting up, he swung Rosa up to perch on his shoulder and took Gabriella by the hand. "After you, Miss Eliza."

The children's looks of wonder at the rooms they passed on the way to the stairs were not lost on Eliza. She crossed her fingers as the small troupe marched up the steps and approached the guest room.

"Well, here we are, angels," Micah said, setting Rosa down and giving her a gentle nudge through the doorway.

"Iss everybody sleepa here?" Gabriella asked, rolling r's in her musical accent. She moved to touch the fluffy counterpane.

"Only you and Rosa," Eliza told her. "This is your bed. My

room is just across the hall. I'll show it to you after while."

"Da door," she said fearfully, "she will be closed?"

"No, sweetheart. We will leave it open, if that's what you'd rather."

During the exchange, her younger sister stuck to Micah like glue, until she spied two rag dolls occupying the rocking chair against the opposite wall. She swung her gaze up at the adults, then hesitantly inched toward the toys, as if expecting to be reprimanded at any moment.

Gabriella obviously knew better than to touch something so pretty. She just held her breath.

Eliza patted her shoulder. "Go right ahead, sweetheart. There's a dolly for each of you."

"For your very own," Micah added emphatically. "To keep."

The beginnings of a real smile tipped up the corners of her lips as she bolted toward the rocker and snatched up the one that wasn't presently being crushed in her sibling's arms. Both children sank to the floor cross-legged and cuddled their new treasures, Gabriella's eyes aglow as she chattered unreservedly to her baby in her mother tongue.

Watching their sweet exuberance, Eliza grew misty-eyed, wishing Rosa, too, would open up. She felt Micah's strong hand clamp onto her shoulder and give a light squeeze.

"So far, so good," he said for her ears alone.

She only nodded.

Micah filled his lungs and strode slowly over to join the girls. Squatting down between them, he drew them into a hug. "I would say these dollies are very happy to have two new friends to look after them and love them. Just like Miss Eliza and Auntie Phoebe want to love you and care for you."

The little ones gazed trustingly up at him.

"But, I'm afraid it's time for me to be going."

Gabriella's eyes welled. She swallowed in alarm. "You com'a back? See us?"

"I sure will, sweetheart. Bright and early tomorrow morning.

We can eat breakfast together. Would you like that?"

"You take us backa home, den?"

He flicked an eloquent glance to Eliza, then looked again into the questioning brown eyes. "Sorry, pumpkin. You know Mrs. Garibaldi isn't able to take care of you anymore. So Miss Eliza is gonna do that for awhile. But it'll be all right; you'll see."

She thought for a second, then gave him a brave nod.

"Meanwhile, you just stay right here as long as you like and have a grand time playing with your dolls."

"And I must go see if my aunt needs help with supper," Eliza added. "I'll come to get you when it's ready."

The little ones exchanged wary glances, but their grudging assent followed fairly quickly.

Eliza and Micah withdrew from the room and started downstairs again.

"Oh, I do hope they get by all right. There's a long night ahead," she said quietly, not wanting her uncertainties to spill over and affect the little ones.

Stopping as they reached the landing, Micah smiled gently. "They've had a pretty tough day. They should be tired early. You'll do fine, believe me. Children can sense a welcoming spirit. In no time at all, you'll have them both wrapped around your little finger."

"Do you really think so?"

"I know it for a fact. Besides, remember all the prayer that's gone into this venture. The Lord is even more concerned about those two tiny fallen sparrows than we are."

"I suppose. Ana was right; you do say the nicest things." But watching his eyes cloud over momentarily, she regretted mentioning her friend's name.

Emitting a weary breath, he finally gave her a half-smile, shrugging one shoulder as he did. "Well, it appears I'll see you tomorrow."

"Bright and early, wasn't it?" she added teasingly. "How

do you like your eggs?"

"Hot."

She rather liked the mischievous sparkle in his eyes, but was sure the static current she felt so often in his presence was a product of her vivid imagination. "Thank you, Micah. . .for everything." With a last glance upstairs, she followed him to the kitchen and watched as he put on his coat and left. Then she let out the breath she'd been holding and went to start some water heating, hoping to persuade the girls to bathe before supper.

When she approached them and mentioned the idea, however, the mere suggestion made the pair skulk against one another and peer at her in disgust as they hugged their dolls tighter.

"We don'a wanna to," Gabriella said, her bottom lip making an appearance as she stubbornly hiked her chin.

"Oh," Eliza hedged, "what a shame. I was hoping you'd want to wear the pretty new nightgowns I bought you." She crossed nonchalantly to the wardrobe and pulled out the soft, long flannel shifts trimmed with ribbon and lace, holding them aloft as she pretended to admire them. "But I know you wouldn't want to spoil them by putting them on over your dirty hair. If you'd rather stay in your present things, that's fine." With an elaborate sigh, she folded the new purchases once more and started to put them back into the drawer.

Gabriella's inner war was almost palpable. Her dark eyes made a once-over circuit of the soiled and patched dresses she and her little sister wore, both obvious hand-me-downs. She drew her lips inward and bit down on them in thought. A small grimace of defeat followed. "We go, eh?" she told her sister. "Take'a da batt." And dutifully, the pair hopped up, trailing behind Eliza as she led them to the bathroom.

From the way they stared at the water closet in passing, it was easy to tell they'd never seen that particular sort of porcelain wonder before, but they quickly became enthralled by Eliza's explanation of its function. And though wary, they even took cautious advantage of the thing. Anything to get the bath siege over and done with as quickly as possible.

Eliza tried not to show her alarm at the sight of their bony ribs and frail frames as she helped them climb into the claw-footed tub of warm water, but she soon had them washed. "My, you both have such curly hair," she said, soaping Gabriella's first. "So nice and thick, too. It'll be really pretty with the ribbons I bought to match your nightgowns."

"Dat'sa nice. We don' haffa da ribbons," the child admitted.

"Well, you do now. They'll look so lovely against your shiny dark curls." Shielding the little girl's eyes with a folded washcloth, she dumped a pitcher of rinse water over her head to wash out the suds.

Gabriella sputtered and wrinkled her nose, but then giggled, which made tackling the same chore with Rosa a mite easier.

To Aunt Phoebe's amazement, two shiny, fragrant little girls appeared at the supper table that night, beribboned, abundant curls spilling over the shoulders of their pristine night shifts, feet clad in soft house slippers. Shy smiles were coming with more frequency. And not long into the meal, so did the yawns.

Seeing that their meager appetites had been sated, Eliza ushered her charges back upstairs, visiting the water closet en route to their bed. "It's been ages since I've had a chance to read a bedtime story to anybody," Eliza commented, turning down the quilts so they could climb in. "I think we'll have one every night you're here."

But before she even reached the midpoint in the account of Noah and the flood, both urchins nodded off. Gazing down at their sweet faces, so innocent in sleep, Eliza's heart crimped. She'd wanted them to hear it all, wanted them to say their prayers afterward, wished they could be part of a whole, happy family again. But all she could do was make it part of her own daily petitions. Putting out the lamp, she paused in the doorway just to look at them for a moment, then went downstairs.

Micah didn't know what to expect when he arrived at Harper House first thing in the morning. The whole place a wreck? Eliza and Mrs. Harper still in their nightclothes, frazzled and in shock, with dark circles under their eyes? A repeat of yesterday's wailing and flailing? Filling his lungs, he rapped on the back door.

"Oh, good morning," Eliza said brightly, admitting him into a kitchen whose enticing smells related the presence of bacon and toasting bread. He heard eggs sizzling in the pan Mrs. Harper was attending on the coal stove and returned the grin she tossed him over her shoulder.

"So, I see you two survived the night," he said casually, hanging his coat.

Eliza's light laughed floated toward him as she set the table for five.

He had to ask. "You had no difficulties whatsoever?"

"Oh, a little crying in the middle of the night, by Rosa," she admitted. "But I went into the room and rocked her for awhile, and she settled back down again. By the way, have you ever heard her talk?" She gestured for him to be seated.

He crossed to the table and tugged out the end chair, lowering himself to it as he shook his head. "I believe she was getting to be quite the little chatterbox until her mama passed away. As far as I know, she hasn't spoken a word since, unless it's been to Gabriella out of anyone else's hearing."

"I wondered."

"Are the girls awake?"

"Those two early birds?" Mrs. Harper chimed in. "They've been skipping up and down the stairs since dawn, the new dollies under their arms. They traipse through here every now and then."

"But they've managed to keep out of mischief?"

Eliza set a cup and saucer before him, then put others out for her and her aunt. "It was part of yesterday's Grand Tour, after you left. I showed them through the whole house, but advised them not to set foot in the gift shop or bother any of Auntie's pretties. And they didn't seem to mind. They had dolls and picture books. They play rather happily in their own room most of the time."

"Well, well. That's good to hear." He took a minute to digest that information while Eliza poured fresh coffee into his cup and passed him the sugar and creamer.

"I believe everything's ready," Aunt Phoebe announced. "Ring the bell, dear." At Micah's surprised expression, she smiled. "Much more pleasant than for us to holler the length of this big house, don't you think?"

No sooner did the tinkly sound fade, then the young charmers came running down the stairs and into the room.

"And who have we here?" he asked in surprise, taking in the brushed and gleaming hair, the dropped-waist dresses with sailor collars and broad sashes. White stockings covered their slim legs, ending in soft-soled house slippers.

Gabriella's eyes flared in delight, and she ran to hug him, little Rosa a mere step or two behind. "We haffa da new dress. Ribbons." Proudly she spun to display the maroon hair ornament that matched her burgundy dress, and her sister mimicked the action in her medium blue ensemble.

"And you look just beautiful." Acknowledging the contrast between the sorry condition they'd been in when he'd first brought them and the spotless, stylish—and smiling—young lasses he saw before him, Micah had only the deepest appreciation for Eliza's rapport with the little ones. Especially when Rosa gravitated to her for help onto a kitchen chair whose low seat had been boosted by the addition of pillows. What a change a loving home made. For certainly this was no less than that.

Since Eliza was otherwise occupied at the moment, he allowed his gaze to linger. Her long hair, instead of being in its loosely woven hair net, was tied at the nape of her slender neck with a velvet ribbon. . .a change he more than liked. Summery blue eyes met his just then, and she smiled. And he had to remind himself to breathe.

❧

"Well, what do you think?" Eliza asked as the youngsters scampered off to play after the meal, leaving the adults to enjoy second cups of coffee at their leisure.

"The word 'speechless' comes to mind," Micah said truthfully. "There's still a trace of the old sadness in their eyes, but it's wonderful to see them smiling again."

"Well, they're such dears," Aunt Phoebe gushed. "When I think of how fearful I was that children would cause nothing but confusion and destruction, I see how foolish an old lady can be. This little pair seems to delight in fairly quiet play. And they're ever so obedient. I must credit their parents for that."

Micah nodded. "That was one thing I observed in my work in the tenements, actually. Even the youngsters living under such deprivation and woeful conditions are for the most part respectful toward adults and cheerful despite life's injustices."

"Yes," Eliza added. "I recall your telling me that many of the families in the tenements were quite well-off in the old country, with respected livelihoods."

"And they often manage to work their way back up to their old standard," he went on, "though it takes a fair amount of time and effort on their part."

"In any event, I truly enjoy looking after these darlings," Eliza said wistfully, "though I'm aware of the great responsibility I've taken on. I know I must endeavor not to allow the girls to become too attached to us, for their own good."

"But while they're here," Aunt Phoebe responded with a grin, "it's a delight to lavish just a bit of attention on them. They've been through so much. Christmas is just around the corner, and I can't help wanting to make it truly nice for them. It may be the first special one they've ever known."

Even as the older woman spoke, Eliza could hear a statement Micah had made not so long ago. *And then what?* Three simple words, yet she couldn't help wondering what the Lord had in store for Gabriella and Rosa Riccio when the joy of Christmastime was past, and they had to settle for real life again, in whatever home or orphanage Micah could find for them.

nineteen

Eliza closed the Bible in her lap and met the little ones' fascinated gazes. "So you see, not only did the Lord take care of all of Joseph's problems in a wonderful way, as we read in last night's story, but He did the same for Ruth. She was no longer poor and lonely. Her faith in the God of her mother-in-law, Naomi, took her to a whole new land, and there God brought another man into her life. One who would love her and become her husband."

"It'sa hard not to feel'a sad when Mama and Papa go to da angels," Gabriella said, her eyes downcast.

"I know, sweetheart. Some things are very difficult for us to understand, especially when loved ones die, as your mama and papa did."

The small curly head nodded.

Sitting on the edge of the children's bed, Eliza leaned over and hugged them both. "It hurts terribly to be left behind. That happened to me when the man who once promised to marry me just went away. I cried a lot, because I knew he didn't really love me after all. But when bad things happen to us, it doesn't ever mean God doesn't love us. He watches over everyone. He even sees when a little bird gets hurt and falls out of the sky. It makes Him sad when we are sad, and He wants to help us and make things better. Even when it feels like things hurt too much, we must learn to trust Him and wait for things to work out again."

"You mean, like'a for Rosa and'a me, God will bring to us da new mama and papa?" Her face scrunched up in question.

"What I'm saying," Eliza explained patiently, "is that God always does what's best for us, when the time is just right."

She turned her face up to Eliza's. "I hope He not'a work too fast, for da new mama. I like'a be wit you. Here. Dis house."

Her younger sister nodded in agreement.

Eliza felt a stinging behind her eyes, and it took a few seconds before she could speak past the huge lump in her throat. "I hope so too, kitten. I love you and Rosa very, very much. But if Mr. Micah finds someone who wants two sweet little girls to be part of their family, we'll all have to remember to trust God. And try to be happy. Even if it's hard at first."

Seeing that her answer seemed to satisfy them, she gathered the girls into her arms and kissed their noses. "But right now I think it's time to say your prayers and go to sleep." Flipping the covers out of the way, she knelt beside the bed, and the two little ones joined her, one on either side, their hands steepled in prayer.

❧

Wide awake as he lay in bed after yet another visit to Harper House, Micah's thoughts still remained there. He'd been stopping by every day since the Italian orphans had taken up temporary residence, and the improvement in their physical appearance was nothing in comparison to the changes in their outlook. He knew Eliza was doing her best to prepare the girls for yet another transition, hoping the next change would go more smoothly. And obviously it was working.

He could also see she was becoming more and more attached to the pair herself. Not uncommon for someone who looked after youngsters who'd been hurt by life's harsh realities. Who didn't wish for the ability to build a place big enough to take in all unwanted and destitute little ones and make everything right for them again?

Anabelle.

He exhaled a painful breath. For all her wonderful qualities, Ana hadn't found that desire, that compassion, within herself. Not that she'd ever kept it a secret. But somehow, that old disappointment didn't matter quite so much as it once had. Micah knew he would always carry a certain kind of love in his heart for his lifelong friend. But he knew she'd done the right thing, the valiant thing, in going away. That's what it had taken for him to see they'd never really been meant for each other. That, and some sleepless, prayer-filled nights. Slowly he'd reached the point of acceptance, the peace that comes from submitting to God's will.

He was still a bit numb inside, aware of an emptiness that would take awhile to fill completely, but he had the calm assurance that the Lord was in control and that "all things work together for good," just as the Bible promised in Romans 8:28.

Latching onto that precious hope, he turned over and closed his eyes, his thoughts drifting pleasantly to a slender, blue-eyed angel who had two sweet little girls under her wings.

❧

Christmas Eve arrived on Saturday, and with it, Micah and his buggy, to pick everyone up for the traditional candlelight service at Faith Community Church. Eliza tried not to notice how his brown checked coat deepened the shade of his eyes, to say nothing of the blatant admiration in them when his gaze meandered to her and stayed for a timeless moment.

"Don't the girls look lovely?" she asked, averting her eyes before she blushed like a silly schoolgirl. She knelt to fasten Rosa's plush velvet cloak, then held the matching muff for the child to slide her hands into while her aunt saw to Gabriella's wrap and warm boots.

Removing his bowler, Micah tipped his head in a gallant gesture which included even Eliza's aunt. "I'll say this. I've never in my life seen a more beautiful group of young ladies all in one place. I'll be the envy of every man at church."

"Oh, pshaw! Everybody puts on their very best for the holiday services." With a cluck of her tongue, Aunt Phoebe took the six-year-old's hand and brushed past him on their way to the door. But not without giving a more-than-pleased grin.

Eliza couldn't help smiling herself.

"Well, that leaves the two of you for me to escort." Micah swept the little one up into the crook of an arm and offered his other elbow to Eliza. "May I?"

"We'd be most honored, sir." Though spoken in a teasing tone, she was all too aware that her insides were quivering like jelly as she took his arm. She hoped it wasn't obvious, but how could anyone notice anything other than the children's glowing eyes anyway? It had been difficult to keep them calm in the face of a special evening, only a prelude to the most wonderful day of the year.

Several inches of new snow had fallen during the afternoon, giving the girls a chance to bundle up and have a romp in the front yard. Now the runners of the sleigh swished over the packed ground cover, and bells on the harness jingled as the horse plodded toward the church, adding an even more festive air.

Once inside the brick building, the sudden warmth from the furnace, along with a multitude of flickering candles lining the front and sides of the sanctuary, stung their cheeks. Micah led the way to an empty pew, nodding in greeting to familiar folks along the way. He stepped aside for Aunt Phoebe, and Gabriella and Eliza filed in behind her. Setting Rosa next to Eliza, he took the aisle seat.

Quiet music from the organ already lent reverence to the occasion, and Eliza fought a twinge of sadness that Anabelle was not at the keys. Though capable enough, the pleasant-faced woman of middle years who had taken her place lacked Ana's natural flair and smooth touch. If Micah shared those sentiments, he did not let on, but Eliza noticed that he avoided looking directly at the big instrument.

She loosened the girls' cloaks, and the two settled back, hands folded in their laps, their attention centered on the large evergreen Christmas tree off to the side, decorated with shining ornaments and candles. It towered over a rough-hewn nativity scene, yet somehow didn't detract from it.

"Da Baby Jesus," Gabriella whispered, pointing out the manger to Rosa, and her sibling craned her neck to see. It was the first time there had been extra objects displayed in the house of worship in the few times Eliza had brought them, and it made them both smile. Often, however, they'd stared in wonder at the empty wooden cross on the wall behind the pulpit.

Though the services contained far less ritual than the little pair were used to, they enjoyed the singing and would sit quietly to the end. Eliza knew they'd particularly like this special one, being mostly made up of carols and the reading of the Christmas story from the Gospel of Luke. It was her own favorite service of the year. This time it seemed all the more touching—whether it was merely having children around for the holidays or having Micah's strong baritone blending with her clear alto, she wasn't about to analyze.

When the program reached the conclusion, the little party bid the pastor and other church members good night, then headed for home.

"It'sa true? What da man say about da Baby Jesus?" Gabriella asked along the way.

"Do you mean that He wasn't always a baby, but that He left heaven to become one just so He could die on the cross for us?" Eliza prompted.

She nodded.

"Yes, sweetheart. God loved us so very much that He sent His only Son to be a sacrifice for our sins. If we know Jesus as our Savior, we know we will go to be with Him when we die."

The tiny frown eased. "I like'a dat. It'sa nice."

Eliza put an arm about Gabriella's small form and hugged her. "Yes. It's very nice."

After reaching home and enjoying some hot chocolate, the girls were tucked in for the night. The busy day had taken its toll. Smiling at the mention of surprises they'd find in the morning, they barely made it through the bedtime story before dropping off to sleep.

Eliza hurried downstairs where she found Micah and her aunt already well into trimming the tree he'd hidden behind the shed earlier that day and brought into the sitting room when she'd gone up with the little ones. The mere thought of the joy it would bring her charges elevated her own anticipation. "That looks ever so lovely," she breathed, assessing their work.

"And won't the little ones love it?" Aunt Phoebe asked, stepping back for an overall view. "Why don't you help Micah finish, while I start gathering the presents to go underneath?"

"*Start* gathering?" Micah echoed good-naturedly. "I hope you two aren't planning on spoiling a certain pair of orphans we all know and love."

"Wel–l–l," the older woman fudged, "they did need so much, you know. But we tried to bear the practical in mind."

"That's good to hear. We wouldn't want to make every Christmas from here on a letdown for them. Their new family might not be so well-off."

Eliza smothered a jolt of alarm. "Does that mean you've found someone willing to take them?" She nearly added "already," but caught herself in time.

As if he sensed her disquiet, he smiled gently and handed her a section of garland to drape around her side of the tree, then moved where he could take it again and continue on his end. "Nothing definite yet. As we all know, there's no shortage of homeless youngsters right now."

It wasn't much as far as reprieves went, but Eliza absorbed what little comfort she could from hearing she wouldn't have to bid Gabriella and Rosa good-bye just yet. Their presence had added so much to this big old house, and she truly hoped they could stay awhile longer. Even Aunt Phoebe appeared years younger and seemed far more energetic and cheerful than she'd been in ages. And with business certain to drop way down after Christmas, the dear woman would have time to spend reading to the girls and making them new treats or clothes.

"Wouldn't you agree?" Micah's voice penetrated her daydreams, and he handed her a brightly painted ornament to hang.

"Hm?" Not quite in her grasp, the shiny teardrop orb slipped to the floor, smashing into a million pieces. "Oh! How clumsy of me." She quickly sank down to gather the remains.

Micah knelt to help. "Tsk, tsk, tsk. Not paying attention, eh? Now you'll be in for it. This was probably a priceless family treasure, too, and now we'll have to mortgage our very souls to replace the thing."

The ridiculous taunt made her laugh. She'd never glimpsed such an embracing light in his eyes, and for a moment she lost herself in it, feeling suddenly warm and giddy and—

Something sharp cut into her palm. With a gasp she snatched her hand from where she'd inadvertently leaned on a fragment of the broken ball.

"Here, let me see," he said at once, taking her hand into his much larger ones. He unraveled the clenched fingers and carefully picked out the tiny shard of colored glass, then used his handkerchief to blot away the few drops of blood that had gathered.

By now more overcome by his tender ministrations than she was by the sting, Eliza watched him with fascination, noticing the play of firelight from the hearth over the lighter strands of his hair, the golden glow it cast upon the planes of his face. Sensations she'd thought had died with the betrayal of her dearest dreams now fluttered through her being, doing indescribable things to her insides.

"I think the patient will live," Micah murmured. Dipping his head as if for one more look, he pressed a light kiss into her palm, then closed her fingers over it. He met her gaze with a heart-stopping smile.

Something she could not name passed between them in

that breathless instant, and for a few seconds she forgot how to breathe. "Th–thank you," was as much of a response as she could generate.

"All part of the service," came his own husky reply.

The soft tapping of Aunt Phoebe's shoes broke the spell as the older woman entered the room and set down an armful of colorfully wrapped gifts. "Oh, what's happened?"

"Nothing much," Eliza blurted a bit too quickly as she struggled to her feet, her face ablaze. "I. . .um. . .broke an ornament. I'm sorry."

Barely giving the shiny remnants more than a cursory glance, she peered from Eliza to Micah with a peculiar smile. "Not to worry. I've always had far too many of those baubles anyway. Well, keep up the good work." And with that, she turned back down the hall.

"I. . .think we're about finished. Don't you?" Eliza said brightly, purposely avoiding looking at Micah again as he put the star atop the tree.

He chuckled. "Yes. . .and no. But I do have to be going. It's getting late, and I must allow you to get whatever sleep you can before our little angels awaken in their roost."

Our. Eliza rather liked the sound of that. A lot. A whole lot. She swallowed. "W–will you come to breakfast?"

"Wouldn't miss it."

"Come as early as you like. We'll let the girls open a present or two beforehand and save the others until after. They'll probably want to wear something new to church."

He nodded. "Sounds good. See you in the morning then. Sleep well, Eliza. I'll find my own way out."

"Well, thanks again. . .for the help, and all."

A soft squeeze to her shoulder, and he strode for the kitchen. A minute more and the back door closed behind him.

Eliza sank to the nearest chair. She could hardly wait for the children to wake up tomorrow.

She could hardly wait for tomorrow—period.

twenty

Somehow, Eliza managed to arise before the children awoke. She told herself it was because she didn't want to miss a second of their wonder upon seeing the sitting room decked out in all its Christmas glory, or the beautiful tree with the pretty packages awaiting them beneath it. Yet all the while, she knew it was more than that.

The memory of last night washed over her, bringing alive Micah's gentleness when he'd tended her cut, the quick wit he was beginning to display with amazing frequency. But surely some of the sensations she'd felt in his presence had to have been the product of her lively imagination. When he arrived shortly she would be much more in control, better able to conduct herself with propriety. Regardless, she was determined to look her very best. For the girls, she avowed.

Not long after she finished her toilette and donned the emerald taffeta gown she'd saved especially for the holiday, she heard whispers and giggles drifting from the room across the hall. Eliza smiled to herself and tiptoed to their doorway. "Good morning, dearies. Merry Christmas."

Four tiny arms hugged her breath away as she bent to embrace them.

"Is'a time to get up'a now?" Gabriella asked in a small voice.

"It is time. Put on your slippers and let's go downstairs. I think I even smell breakfast—and here I thought we were the first ones awake. Isn't that silly?"

The girls giggled. Hopping out of bed, they did as told, then latched onto Eliza's hands.

The fragrant scent of the pine boughs which had been

hung here and there about the first floor grew stronger as she and the girls descended the stairs. Partway down, Gabriella glimpsed the tree and some of the other decorations adorning the sitting room. She caught her breath. Wide-eyed, she tugged her fingers free and scampered the rest of the way, pausing just inside the doorway to stare.

Eliza and Rosa joined her within seconds, and the little ones beamed with delight when Micah and Aunt Phoebe also came from the kitchen. Eliza lowered her lashes.

"Is'a so. . .so. . ." Unable even to express herself in English, Gabriella grabbed Eliza and started pulling her closer to the lovely tree.

"Yes, it's ever so pretty," Eliza finished for her, warming under Micah's gaze. "And some of these nice presents are for you and Rosa."

Her chocolate-brown eyes widened. She stole a peek at her sister, and the two of them squealed.

"You may open one or two now, and after breakfast we'll all come back in here for the rest."

No other invitation was needed, as instantly the little ones chose tempting-looking packages and began tearing into them, Gabriella discovering a warm sweater and a coloring book with colored pencils; Rosa finding a new dress and a ball.

The length of time it took for them to put down the first items and take up the second touched Eliza deeply. For children who'd had so little, everything was appreciated.

A pancake breakfast followed, with the girls almost too animated to eat. But the adults prevailed upon them to finish their portions.

Returning to the sitting room afterward, a pair of dainty little basket cradles Aunt Phoebe had fixed up for the girls' dollies were a great hit, as were new gloves and church dresses. They touched their new bounty with reverent fingers and hugged each one in turn. And Gabriella planted a huge kiss on Micah's cheek in thanks for the new picture books he'd brought.

"Oh, you're not quite finished yet," Eliza said, kneeling to reach below the bottommost branches of the tree for two more boxes. She held them out, and the girls happily came to get them.

Ripping into hers, Gabriella removed the lid and peered inside. "Ohhh." Her mouth dropped open as she pulled out some new, laced, high-top shoes for everyday and a pair with dainty buckles for Sundays. Then she caught her lower lip in her teeth and burst into tears.

Eliza flew to her side and stooped beside her. "But what is wrong, sweetheart? Don't you like them?"

At this, the little girl wailed even louder, throwing her arms around Eliza as she collapsed in wrenching sobs.

Eliza didn't know what to think and looked at Aunt Phoebe and Micah for answers, but they appeared as flabbergasted as she. There was nothing to do but wait it out. And when the weeping evolved into watery smiles, everyone was thoroughly confused.

"I. . .I. . .*graci,*" Gabriella choked out at last as she eased from Eliza's embrace. "Da shoes, dey'sa new. Always'a we get old'a shoes, Rosa, me. Too big. Too small. First time'a new. *Graci. Graci.*" And she crossed to hug Aunt Phoebe—the older woman unabashedly wiping her own cheeks—and Micah, who couldn't even speak.

Eliza, too, had been reduced to tears, but the short span provided a chance to dig out her handkerchief and recover a bit. And the sight of Rosa hobbling around in one of each of her new footwear provided some comic relief.

"Well," her aunt said at length, patting Micah's knee and smiling at Eliza. "I don't know about you two, but I almost don't care what we'll find in our packages."

"I couldn't have said it better myself," he replied. "Why don't we wait till later? I'd just as soon drink in the wonder of those young faces for awhile." He averted his gaze to the children playing with their new toys.

"I'll go put on a fresh pot of coffee," the old woman offered. "It'll soon be time for church."

❧

The afternoon passed fairly quickly, and by the time it ended, all the grown-ups had entered into playacting with Gabriella and Rosa at one time or another. Aunt Phoebe pretended to be the dollies' grandmother and helped change and dress the babies; Micah read over and over to them from the books he'd brought, plus sat on the floor too with Rosa to roll her new ball back and forth; and Eliza rediscovered her love of coloring.

Finally, after partaking of a veritable feast the two women had prepared, the children actually asked if they could go to bed. "Go on," Aunt Phoebe told Eliza. "I'll clean up here." And a noticeable quiet settled over Harper House, one so still that Eliza's light steps could be heard on her return downstairs.

"My. What a day." She sank wearily into an overstuffed chair in the sitting room, where Micah was stoking up the fire in the hearth after adding some new logs.

He grinned over his shoulder. "I'll say. Longer than usual, too. I feel like I've been up forever."

"I think we all have. Thank you for coming to help make Christmas special for Gabriella and Rosa. And for the lovely necklace watch. It's simply exquisite."

"I hoped you'd like it. And I'll enjoy the devotional book and the new gloves from you. Thanks." Finished with his task, he brushed off his hands and took a chair across from Eliza.

"And wasn't my aunt's gift rather sweet? Imagine, that carved chest—which she alleges is only my first Epiphany gift."

"Yes, she's been in her element, coming up with surprises for the lot of us. She's recovered amazingly well from that last spell since the little ones have been here."

Eliza smiled. "She's doted on them every spare minute, and they get along wonderfully with Aunt Phoebe."

"Did I hear my name?" the silver-haired woman asked, drying her hands on a kitchen towel as she came into the room.

"Oh, we were just mentioning how well you've managed to cope with the girls' presence."

"Hmph. I daresay, I've done more than cope. It's been a downright pleasure to do for those two. They've got a lot of love to give. It's a crying shame they were left with nobody to give it to."

"Oh, now," Micah cajoled. "Looks to me like they're not having any trouble at all passing their love around. In many ways, their sad loss has turned out to be a blessing."

"For us, perhaps. And I'm not at all in a hurry for you to plunk them in with another bunch of strangers, so you just take your time doing that, if you can." She gave a tired sigh. "Anyway, I was just finishing up in the kitchen and thought I'd see if there's anything you two wanted before I turn in. I've about walked these old feet off and need to put them up."

Eliza rose and went to hug her. "No, Auntie, you've done quite enough. If there's anything we want, I'm perfectly capable of seeing to it. You just have a good rest. Tomorrow's another day."

"Yes, dear lady," Micah added. "You've worked much harder than any of us deserved. Thank you for the hospitality—and the leather case for my papers. I'll put that to good use, believe me."

She looked from one of them to the other and smiled. "Well, good night, then. And Merry Christmas."

Within seconds of the almost-inaudible click of her aunt's bedroom door latch, Eliza became aware of a sudden change in the atmosphere. The crackling of the fire was the only sound in the room. In the whole house, for that matter. She ventured a look in Micah's direction.

His gaze was centered on her, his expression unreadable.

She cleared her throat. "Would you care for some tea? Coffee?"

"Not especially, thanks."

Taking another tack to calm her growing nervousness, Eliza settled on a safe subject. "The girls had a truly delightful day today, far beyond what I'd even hoped."

Micah's eyes gentled with his smile. "Yes. Just watching them, witnessing their genuine thankfulness, was quite humbling, I must say. The rest of us, we take a lot for granted. They helped put things back into perspective for me."

"For me, as well." She paused. "I. . .I don't know how I'll ever find strength to give them up when the time comes. I didn't mean to become so attached. In fact, I tried very hard not to. But now—"

"I know," he said gently. "I've been watching it happen. But you're only human, Eliza. How could a person open up her home to those less privileged, unless possessing of a heart easily touched by the need? And look at those two, for pity's sake. Those big doe eyes, the trust and vulnerability, the honesty. It's a combination impossible to resist."

Neither spoke for a short span.

"You look very beautiful today," Micah said at length. "Is that a new gown? I don't believe I've seen it before."

"It's from my trou—I mean, yes. I've been saving it." Fighting a maddening blush, she gave a silent huff at her near blunder. She'd been so stupid—first for imagining she loved Weston and then for comparing him to Micah. Why, just looking at him, anyone could see Micah's face was not so long, his features were much more noble and expressive, his eyes—they were so much more compelling, so. . .*near.*

He had gotten up and now stood before her.

"Come here," he said, holding out his hand to her.

Eliza knew her knees couldn't possibly support her right now. She would collapse at his feet in a heap, and he'd have to pick her up. But as she placed her fingers in his, she felt his strength flow into her being, enabling her to stand.

"We almost missed a very important part of Christmas," he

said, those hazel eyes challenging hers unmercifully.

Having no idea what he was talking about, Eliza nevertheless let him draw her toward the hallway.

But rather than leave the sitting room altogether, he stopped at the arch marking the entrance to it and smiled.

"What are you doing?" she asked, thoroughly confused now.

His gaze traveled upward.

Hers followed. And stopped directly above her head.

"Mistletoe!"

"A very important part of Christmas," he said again.

Every fiber of her being turned to liquid, and her heart raced as he turned her to face him.

"I've been waiting all day for this moment," he whispered. He was not teasing now, and his smile faded as his eyes searched hers, waiting for her reaction. Giving her time to pull away, if that's what she wanted.

What she wanted, she realized, was for this moment to be real. More than just a Christmas kiss. But dared she hope for that? Throwing caution to the wind, she leaned toward him ever so slightly, her lips parted.

With a smothered groan, Micah encircled her in his strong arms and lowered his head. His lips met hers in a kiss that was joyous, reverent, passionate, promising. And over too soon.

"Oh, Micah," she whispered breathlessly, her cheek pressed to his chest, knowing he must feel her heart thundering against her ribs. As she could feel his.

He cupped the back of her head, rocking her for a moment in his arms. "I think I've known for some time that I was falling in love with you," he admitted. "But I tried to convince myself I was wrong. I don't want to be wrong anymore, Eliza."

She lifted her head and raised her lashes to look into those soulful eyes she loved.

"And I know you've been hurt before," he continued. "So I promise I won't rush you. But I'm asking for permission to court you, if you'll allow me to."

Her heart soared, but she wasn't about to interrupt. Not now. Not for anything.

"I don't have a lot to offer you right now, but I have plans and dreams I've never shared with anyone. Dreams I believe you could be a part of, if you'll only trust me."

Eliza felt a smile moving across her lips.

"Will you please say something?" he finally pleaded.

"For your information, Micah Richmond, I have quite a lot to say. That was quite a speech."

"It wasn't just a speech. I meant every word."

She placed a palm along his face, loving his warmth, loving the feel of him, almost beyond herself at God's goodness. She had gotten up this morning hoping the day would be one Gabriella and Rosa would always remember, never once entertaining the hope that it would be special for her, too. But Micah had made it so. Micah and Aunt Phoebe, and the girls, all together. And then came the heartfelt touches brought by little shoes and mistletoe. Her being could scarcely contain her happiness.

"I know you meant it, Micah," she said softly. "Your heart told me it was all truc."

His face brightened as a hope-filled grin spread from ear to ear.

"So, yes, I will trust you. Because, yes, I love you, too. And it would be my great honor to hear more about all those dreams of yours."

"Well," he began, "my dearest dream has been to have someone I could share them with. So come with me, my love." He led her toward the sitting room once more. "I hardly know where to begin."

With her hand in his, Eliza felt supreme peace at last. A peace that brought with it a gentle conviction that God had already begun to work all things together for good. . . this was His time.

epilogue

"Mama, Mama! Papa, he comes!" Rosa skipped up the steps of the big Richmond house and into the parlor, long curls askew from play, her arms golden-brown from the summer sun. "He'sa bring a lady."

Moving to peer outside through the lace window shade, Eliza smiled with recognition and lumbered to the door with as much haste as possible, a hand on her rounded abdomen. She waited on the broad front porch for the buggy to draw to a stop.

Gabriella, who always ran ahead to latch on to the side and ride from the corner, hopped down from the vehicle's step and stood while Micah got out and gave a hand to his stylish blond passenger. A tall man of medium build alighted last and linked a proprietary elbow through the woman's before the small troupe came up the walk.

"Anabelle!" Eliza exclaimed as her friend, ever so fashionable in her leg-o'mutton-sleeved gray jacket and matching skirt, swept up the steps.

"Eliza, dear." She withdrew her arm and came to grab Eliza in a huge hug. "Ned and I are just now returning from our honeymoon in Europe. Micah happened along the quay as we were arranging transport—"

"And insisted they make their first stop here," Micah finished. Beside him, Gabriella smiled, appearing quite the young lady as she gazed from one adult to the other.

"Well, I'm so glad you did." Eliza stepped back to assess Ana's slender form. "You look simply marvelous!"

"And so do you." Anabelle patted Eliza's tummy with a smile and leaned close to whisper in her ear. "I think I might be joining the ranks of motherhood soon myself." But she put a finger to her lips before turning around. "You really must meet my husband. Ned?" She turned adoring eyes on him.

The finely attired young gentleman stepped forward, removing the bowler from his auburn head, silver-gray eyes obviously glowing with pride as they fastened on his wife. His reddish mustache quirked with a smile.

"Ned, love, I'd like you to meet my other dearest friend in the world, Eliza Richmond. Eliza, my husband, Ned Fairbanks."

"It's an honor," he said pleasantly. "I've heard so much about you."

"Very pleased to meet you," Eliza said, offering a hand which he clasped warmly. "You both must be tired from traveling. I'll put on some tea."

"I'll help, Mama." Gabriella opened the door for them, while Micah took Ned on a tour of the grounds, Rosa tagging along with her papa.

"My," Ana gushed when they reached the kitchen. She took a chair and glanced casually about the tidy workroom, observing Gabriella's quiet movements as the child took cups down from the cupboard. "You've got a ready-made family."

"Yes. We've had our two sweet girls for a couple years now. Actually, they were the first residents in that guest room you helped me fix up at Aunt Phoebe's. Auntie's looking after an infant now, a little boy, while Micah finalizes matters for the family who will adopt him."

"You don't say. How interesting."

Eliza smiled. "But my heart went out to this pair from the start. We couldn't imagine being without them." She brushed one of Gabriella's silken curls behind the girl's shoulder and was rewarded with a tender smile.

"It's wonderful to know this grand old house is back in Micah's hands, too," Anabelle remarked. "So many memories. And now you and he will be making new ones."

Nodding as she poured their tea, Eliza met Ana's green eyes. "Are you as happy as you look, Anabelle?"

"I've never been more so," she answered honestly. "My Ned's a wonderful man, kind, thoughtful, and he is quite gifted musically. We're often invited to churches to perform on the organ and violin." She paused. "And I needn't ask if you and Micah are happy. I can see that for myself. I knew all along you'd be marvelous together."

"All the same, I know it took a lot of love for you to give him up," Eliza said. "I will always be grateful to you for that."

"I won't pretend it was easy, but I've not regretted it. The Lord had someone else in mind for me, my soul mate."

"And have you come back to the city for good now?"

Anabelle shook her head, her straw bonnet moving slightly with her movements. "Only for the next few months. Then Ned will take up a position teaching music at a school in Boston. But we'll be staying at Mother's until then."

"Oh, well, we can get together for awhile, at least."

"Yes. I doubt there's a greater blessing than friendship. I'm truly looking forward to renewing ours again."

"So am I."

The sound of clomping footsteps carried from the back porch.

"And here come those husbands of ours. Gabi, would you mind getting out a few more cups? We want our friends to tell us all about Europe and the wondrous sights they saw while they were there." But Eliza knew the most wonderful sight was the love between friends and family together at last.

A Letter To Our Readers

Dear Reader:

In order that we might better contribute to your reading enjoyment, we would appreciate your taking a few minutes to respond to the following questions. We welcome your comments and read each form and letter we receive. When completed, please return to the following:

Rebecca Germany, Fiction Editor
Heartsong Presents
PO Box 719
Uhrichsville, Ohio 44683

1. Did you enjoy reading *Little Shoes and Mistletoe?*
   - ❑ Very much. I would like to see more books by this author!
   - ❑ Moderately
   I would have enjoyed it more if ________________

   ____

   ____

2. Are you a member of **Heartsong Presents**? Yes ❑ No ❑
   If no, where did you purchase this book? ______________

   ____

3. How would you rate, on a scale from 1 (poor) to 5 (superior), the cover design? ________________________

4. On a scale from 1 (poor) to 10 (superior), please rate the following elements.

   _____ Heroine _____ Plot

   _____ Hero _____ Inspirational theme

   _____ Setting _____ Secondary characters

5. These characters were special because________________

____

____

6. How has this book inspired your life?________________

____

____

7. What settings would you like to see covered in future **Heartsong Presents** books?__________________

____

____

8. What are some inspirational themes you would like to see treated in future books?__________________

____

____

9. Would you be interested in reading other **Heartsong Presents** titles? Yes ❑ No ❑

10. Please check your age range:
❑ Under 18 ❑ 18-24 ❑ 25-34
❑ 35-45 ❑ 46-55 ❑ Over 55

11. How many hours per week do you read?______________

Name ____

Occupation ______________________________________

Address ____

City _______________ State ___________ Zip ___________